# It's another Quality Book from CGP

This book is for 11-14 year olds doing KS3 History.

As well as learning skills and ideas, there are lots of facts
in History and you've just got to learn them.

Happily this CGP book gives you all that important
information as clearly and concisely as possible.

It's also got some daft bits in to try and make the whole
experience at least vaguely entertaining for you.

# What CGP is all about

Our sole aim here at CGP is to produce the highest quality books
— carefully written, immaculately presented and dangerously
close to being funny.

Then we work our socks off to get them out to you
— at the cheapest possible prices.

# Contents

## Section Three — The Making of Modern Britain

## Section Four — The Rest Of The World

Published by Coordination Group Publications Ltd.

*Contributors:*
Steve Buckley
Mark Chambers
Rene Cochlin
Taissa Csaky
Matt Hardwick
John Pritchard
Katherine Reed
James Paul Wallis
Chrissy Williams
Henry I
Henry II
and Henry VIII
(the others couldn't make it)

ISBN 1 84146 330 2

Groovy website: www.cgpbooks.co.uk
Jolly bits of clipart from CorelDRAW
Printed by Elanders Hindson, Newcastle upon Tyne.

With thanks to Angela Ryder for the proofreading.

# The Norman Conquest and Beyond

Just after Harold became King of England (King of the Saxons), some Vikings invaded at Stamford Bridge. Harold won, but then William of Normandy said he should be the King, and invaded Britain.

## William Invaded, and Won the Battle of Hastings

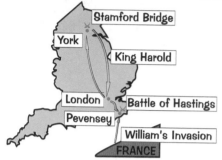

Stamford Bridge
York
King Harold
London
Pevensey
Battle of Hastings
William's Invasion
FRANCE

Harold <u>marched</u> his <u>tired army</u> back south to meet William, getting a few more soldiers on the way.
1) William moved his army to <u>Hastings</u>.
2) Harold positioned his army to <u>block the road</u> to London.
3) William now had to <u>attack</u> if he wanted to become king.
The <u>Battle of Hastings</u> was fought on <u>October 14<sup>th</sup> 1066</u>.
William's army was <u>well trained</u> and had lots of <u>knights</u>.
Harold had about the <u>same number</u>, but they were all <u>tired foot soldiers</u>.

1) William tried archers first, then spearmen and then knights.
2) Nothing seemed to be working. Then he got lucky — his <u>Breton allies ran away</u> and some of the <u>Saxons followed them</u>, leaving fewer to fight against William.
3) The Normans rode them down, the Saxon line was now thinner.
4) The Norman archers could now <u>shoot at the Saxons</u>.
5) The knights charged the Saxons and Harold was killed — William had won.

The Normans made the <u>Bayeux Tapestry</u> to show what they said happened.

## Being King of England Wasn't Easy

William was crowned King on <u>Christmas Day 1066</u>, but his problems were just starting.

1) William <u>built castles</u> to try and take control of the country.
2) William ordered the <u>Domesday Book</u> to record everything about England, and to see how much tax he should be given (more about this on p2).
3) There were three <u>serious rebellions</u> against his rule which he put a stop to — in the North, the South West and in East Anglia.
4) In 1069 some Vikings and northern English men rebelled against William. They failed but William was worried, so he <u>burned and destroyed</u> everything in the <u>North</u>.

## William's Son became the Next King

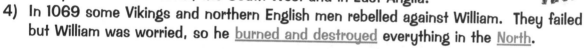

William the Conqueror died in 1087 after a riding accident. The new King was his son, <u>William Rufus</u>. He was known as Rufus because of his red/ruddy complexion (Rufus means "red" in Latin).
1) Rufus took control of the English throne.
2) Rufus's reign was bloody, but not a total failure. He <u>taxed</u> people as much as he could and <u>beat off foreign invaders</u> and revolts at home.
3) He conquered <u>Cumbria</u> and <u>Wales</u> and overthrew the <u>Scottish King</u>.
4) Some of his <u>Barons rebelled</u> in support of his brother Robert, but he <u>beat them off</u> too.
5) In <u>1100</u>, Rufus was shot in the back on a hunting trip. Some people think that the chief suspect (Walter Tyrel) was obeying orders from the King's younger brother, Henry, who became king next.

## Learn from history — don't play with arrows...

William I built the Tower of London and Windsor Castle you know. Ah — I miss the good old days, when people didn't so much "go on holiday" as conquer a country and build themselves a castle.

# What The Domesday Book Tells Us

Twenty years after the Battle of Hastings, William the Conqueror decided to discover who really owned all the land in England. This was basically so he could work out who owed him taxes...

## The Domesday Book Was Not Popular

The Domesday Book was basically a big list of who owned what in England. William I used it to calculate how much to tax people. So, clearly everyone was a bit gutted about this. It was written in 1086 and asked questions like —
1) How many slaves and freemen are there in your manor?
2) How much is your manor worth?
It even recorded things like how many animals you had on your land. It showed how efficient the Normans were, compared to the Saxons who ruled before them.

no pigs here

## The Domesday Book Tells us about Village Life

*There were Norman Kings in Sicily as well as England. Wow. Bet that's a bit nicer than Grimsby on a cold winter's morning.*

The Domesday Book gives us a pretty good picture of life in the country —
1) The overall population was around one and a half million people, and 90-95% of people lived in rural areas.
2) Villages were small — around 300-500 people.
3) There were often one or two manors in a village (manors were basically big fortified houses that looked like castles), where a Lord or Baron lived.
4) Peasants living in the villages were mostly "villeins".
5) Villeins had their own small pieces of land to farm, but to pay for them they had to work on the Lord of the Manor's land as well. A system like this where you pay for land with work (not money) is called a feudal system. It makes the landowners very powerful.
6) Villeins had three chances of freedom — they could receive it from the Lord of the Manor, save up enough to buy it, or else run away to a town and if they weren't caught for a year and a day then they became free.

## The Domesday Book Also Tells us about Town Life

Only 100 towns were included in the Domesday Book.
1) The only big places were around cathedrals, such as Lincoln, York and Westminster Abbey.
2) Towns developed around travel and meeting points such as crossroads or river crossings.
3) Towns attracted villagers and merchants to trade.
4) Craftsmen and merchants formed guilds to protect the quality of their work.
5) Wealthy towns built large defensive walls.
6) Successful towns gained charters setting out the rights of townspeople. These were awarded by the Lord or bought from the King.

Westminster Abbey —
Great Gothic Architecture...

## "Argh, we're all doomed" — "Oh be quiet it's only a book..."

All this feudal system malarky sounds weird to me. Are you really telling me that if you were a peasant, your best shot at freedom was running away from home and hiding out in a dung-infested town for a year and a day? What a nightmare. I've seen the pictures. Those places look smelly.

# Relations With Other Countries

At the start of the Middle Ages, England looked to Scandinavia for friends and enemies — by the end, France and Ireland were much more important to foreign policy.

## The English Kings Tried to Conquer All of Britain

### Ireland

1) The English first got involved in Ireland when Dermot McMurrough (King of Leinster) lost his throne, and asked Henry II to help him get it back.
2) Henry was offered an oath of fealty by Dermot in return for his help (fealty = an oath of loyalty and obedience to the king).
3) Henry built castles and sent knights to hold onto his claims.
4) Most Irish chieftains seemed quite happy with this.
5) Henry VIII was the first English king to call himself "King of Ireland" (in the early 1500s) — up until then the Irish chieftains gave allegiance to the King of England, but still did what they wanted.

### Scotland

There was a lot of argument about whether Scotland was a free country. The English thought the Scots owed them an oath of loyalty, but not all the Scots agreed.

1) Edward I, the "Hammer of the Scots", conquered Scotland at the end of the 1200s.
2) However, Robert the Bruce freed Scotland by 1328.
3) Throughout the Middle Ages there were lots of border raids (and general mischief) between the English and Scots.

### Wales

1) The Normans took over bits of Wales when they first conquered England. But, because of the mountains, Wales was hard to control.
2) Edward I conquered Wales in the 1270s and 80s and built concentric castles to control it.
3) Though there were still many revolts against the English, Wales was under English control by Henry VII's day in around 1500.

## Wars with France went on for 100 Years

When the Normans conquered England in 1066, they already controlled a large part of France. Henry II controlled Normandy and Anjou, then he married Eleanor of Aquitaine and added Aquitaine to his French Empire. But by 1216 much of this land had been lost by King John.

1) In 1337 Edward III invaded France to take back his lands in France, the war would last about 116 years.
2) The English archers, armed with longbows, won victories at Crecy in 1346, Poitiers in 1356 and Agincourt in 1415.
3) But the war was expensive and by 1453 the English had lost everything but Calais.

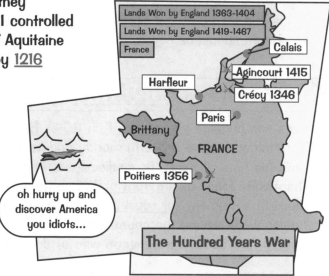

Lands Won by England 1363-1404
Lands Won by England 1419-1467
France
Calais
Harfleur
Agincourt 1415
Crécy 1346
Paris
Brittany
FRANCE
Poitiers 1356

oh hurry up and discover America you idiots...

The Hundred Years War

## And now for the famous bit...

Joan of Arc was a teenage, French, peasant girl who saw visions which told her to free France from the English. The French leader, who must have been a bit desperate, let her help lead the army. She had a victory at Orléans, but ended up being captured and burnt by the English in 1431.

# Matilda, Stephen and Henry II

Right — Henry I was King after William II. Then he went and left the throne to his daughter Matilda. That's right — a GIRL. Not a lot of people liked that.

## Monarchs **Were Expected to be** Male

1) Monarchs were expected to maintain <u>law and order</u> in the kingdom.
2) Monarchs were expected to be <u>blokes</u> — lots of people back then thought women shouldn't be in positions of power.
3) Monarchs had to control the unruly and power hungry <u>groups of barons</u> that they relied upon for support. Most of these barons didn't believe women should rule.

Henry I was a strong monarch, but in 1120 a boat called <u>The White Ship</u> sank — Henry's sons were on it. His sons <u>drowned</u>, leaving Henry grief-stricken and with no male heir.

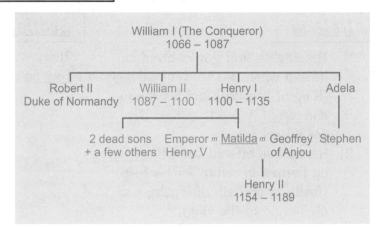

## Matilda didn't **get to be** Queen

1) <u>Matilda</u> was <u>betrothed</u> to the German <u>Holy Roman Emperor</u> when she was 8.
2) When he died in 1125, her dad Henry ordered her to marry <u>Geoffrey of Anjou</u>.
3) In 1126 Henry got all the English lords, including his nephew Stephen, to <u>acknowledge Matilda</u> as his <u>heir</u>.
4) Henry died in 1135. BUT, Matilda's cousin <u>Stephen</u> got to <u>London</u> before Matilda did, and had himself <u>crowned king</u>.
5) Most nobles wanted <u>Stephen</u> to rule, because he was a <u>man</u>.
6) This basically started off a <u>civil war</u> that lasted for nearly twenty years. <u>Neither side won</u>. Stephen wasn't ruthless enough, and Matilda was a bit too vicious and alienated most of her supporters. She ruled for about 8 months, but it was as '<u>Lady of the English</u>', not Queen.
7) In the end they both got bored and decided that Stephen could <u>remain king</u>, but that <u>Matilda's son</u> Henry should be <u>heir</u> to the throne (Stephen didn't have any sons of his own).

*Stephen had Matilda trapped in Oxford Castle, but she managed to escape by putting on a white robe and legging it during a snow storm.*

## Henry II Revamped **the** Court System

Matilda's son became <u>King Henry II</u> in <u>1154</u>. He's remembered in general as having been intelligent and determined (and also pretty moody and mean). He <u>reformed the court system</u>.
1) Until the time of Henry II, medieval courts were really <u>disorganised</u> and <u>complicated</u>.
2) There were loads of <u>different courts</u> competing for power (e.g. church courts, manor courts).
3) Henry II set up <u>regular royal courts</u> to deal with serious offences such as murder.
4) Judges went around the country to <u>hold trials</u>.
5) <u>Trial by jury</u> became a common way of deciding who was guilty, and things got a lot fairer.

## Henry II — dunno, I don't normally like sequels...

Henry II was the first <u>Plantagenet</u> King. (Plantagenet was his dad's nickname because he used to wear a "planta genista" sprig in his hat.) The name "Plantagenet" wasn't actually used by the royal family till about 300 years later though. Lots of historians use the word "Angevins" instead (because Henry's dad was Geoffrey of <u>Anjou</u>). So there. Are you having fun yet?

# Henry II, Richard I and King John

Henry II got his friend Thomas à Becket the job of Archbishop of Canterbury. Henry was hoping this'd mean the church and the crown would get along okay. But nothing's ever that easy...

## Henry and Thomas Couldn't Agree on Anything

1) Henry and Thomas argued over whether the church should be part of the kingdom, or whether it should have its own separate powers.
2) One major issue was about how criminal priests should be punished. Henry thought they should be dealt with by the royal courts, but Thomas reckoned the church should have its own courts.
3) One day Henry angrily cried out to his knights, asking them how they could "allow their lord to be treated with such shameful contempt"? (NOT, as the legend goes, "who will rid me of this turbulent priest?")
4) In any case, four of his knights took that as an instruction to murder Thomas à Becket. So they went off and murdered him on the steps of Canterbury Cathedral in 1170.
5) Becket was made a saint, and in 1174, Henry himself went on a pilgrimage to the shrine. He walked up to it barefoot, fell on his face (on purpose), confessed his sins and was whipped five times each by the surrounding monks. He stayed there all night, fasting, surrounded by pilgrims.

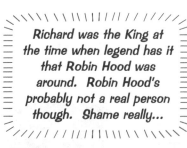

*Richard was the King at the time when legend has it that Robin Hood was around. Robin Hood's probably not a real person though. Shame really...*

## King Richard was a Brave Man

1) Henry II had four kids. The oldest, Richard, was the next king and after that came his brother John.
2) Richard I fought lots of crusades in the Holy Lands.
3) He spent less than a year in England in the 10 years he was king.
4) He's gone down in history as a brave, strong, brilliant warrior king. He left the country in a bit of a state for his brother John though...

## But John was a Moody Old So and So

Richard spent all England's money on the crusades. This left John a bit stuck.

1) John needed money in order to pay soldiers to fight wars for him.
2) John had lost his lands in France and wanted them back, but not all the barons were in favour of an expensive war.
3) John also fell out with the Pope in Rome, over who should be the next Archbishop of Canterbury. The Pope excommunicated John (i.e. he expelled him from the church) and declared that he wasn't the rightful king of England.
4) John also overtaxed the barons, and it wasn't long before they rebelled against him.

## John signed the Magna Carta

The rebelling barons forced John to meet them in a field at Runnymede and sign the Magna Carta in 1215. Magna Carta means 'Great Charter', and it centred around three main points —

1) The English church would be free from state control (i.e. from the King's control) at last.
2) No freeman could be arrested, imprisoned or executed without a fair trial.
3) The king couldn't raise taxes without the agreement of Barons and Bishops first.

There were over 63 clauses in total, and the Magna Carta laid the foundation for British democracy.

## Go and see the Magna Carta in Salisbury Cathedral...

You can date people by which Robin Hood film they watched as a kid. I was lumbered with the rubbish Kevin Costner version. My gran still swoons for Errol Flynn. I reckon a new one is in order*.

* Starring, ooh, Orlando Bloom as Robin...

# The Black Death

Okay — now we can't be sure exactly how many people died because of the Black Death, but it might have been as many as <u>half</u> of the whole British population. That's a LOT of people.

## 33-50% of the Population Died

1) Plague probably killed between a third and half of the <u>total population</u> of the British Isles.
2) Bubonic plague was <u>spread by fleas</u> which were carried by black rats.
3) Pneumonic plague affected the lungs and <u>breathing</u>. Some historians suggest other diseases were also involved — for example anthrax.
4) Many people were already weakened due to <u>poor harvests</u> and famine caused by poor summer weather.

Summer 1348 — Bubonic plague travels across the south of England
September 1348 — Plague hits London
January 1349 — Parliament decides to stop meeting
Spring 1349 — Plague now spread into East Anglia, along Coast, Wales, and Midlands
Summer 1349 — Plague hits the North and Ireland
1349 — The Scots raid Durham while England is weak
1350 — The plague hits Scotland but eases off in London
1361-64, 1368, 1371, 1373-75, 1390, 1405 — Plague comes back

## People had Different Explanations for the Black Death

People in medieval times had no idea about germs — they had their own explanations.

1) Some people thought it was an <u>act of God</u>, and that they were being punished for their sins. People thought their very way of life was being punished.
2) Some people were very <u>superstitious</u>, and thought it was the result of a curse or an evil spirit.
3) Some people thought they were being <u>poisoned</u>. Individuals, or different groups were blamed. e.g. Jews, the poor.

**BEFORE**

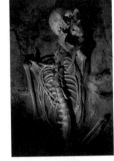
**AFTER**

## It Made Life Better for the Survivors

*The story of <u>3 Kings and the 3 Skeletons</u> tells how 3 kings went into a town thinking they were safe from the plague, but met 3 skeletons who had been kings, and so they realised they were in danger.*

1) Initially some people <u>blamed the poor</u> for the Black Death. It took a while for the King and the nobility to realise that it would affect them too.
2) Killing off so much of the population did actually <u>make life better</u> for the majority of people in the end because it made the survivors <u>more valuable</u>.
3) Before the plague struck, poor people had been <u>forced</u> to work on their local Lord's land, but now they could ask for extra wages and better treatment.
4) It speeded up the breakdown and end of the feudal system, and meant that the <u>ordinary peasants</u> had more <u>freedom</u>.

## The black death — bad for your health...

The symptoms were nasty — sweating, fever, coughing, sneezing, problems breathing. Lumps of poison would appear in your armpits and groin. Eugh. If you were lucky you died in 1 or 2 days. Some people spent 5 or 6 days in total agony. Makes having your tonsils out seem okay, doesn't it?

# *1381 Peasants' Revolt*

In 1381 just about everything was going wrong — bit of a nightmare really. Loads of people had died from the Black Death. The peasants were really fed up, so they rebelled. Hoorah for them.

## *No One Wanted to Be Bossed Around Anymore*

1) The feudal system was collapsing. Feudal dues were being replaced by money-rent systems. (See p2 for a reminder about the feudal system).

2) The Black Death had led to a shortage of workers, (because half of them died), and peasant labour was in high demand.

3) The peasants thought this was pretty cool — they had some privileges now.

4) Some peasants were forced to work for the Church. These peasants had to work without pay, as it was thought that they were doing 'God's work'.

5) Also, everyone had to pay tithes (i.e. taxes) to the Church — one tenth of everything they produced or earned.

6) Most people (even landowners) were unhappy that Bishops were so wealthy, while normal people had to pay loads of taxes.

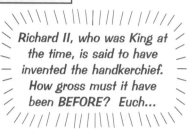

Richard II, who was King at the time, is said to have invented the handkerchief. How gross must it have been BEFORE? Euch...

Put that axe down and get yourself a tissue.

## *The Raising of Taxes Made Everyone Mad*

John of Gaunt was King Richard II's uncle. Richard was only 10 when he became King, so John ruled for him. He kept introducing more taxes to pay for the army. Everyone started to get angry —

1) 1377 — John introduced a Poll Tax in order to finance a war with France. Everyone over 15 years old had to pay 4 pence (not much now, but it would have been a pretty big deal then).

2) 1379 — John introduced a second Poll Tax that asked for more money.

3) 1381 — A third Poll Tax was introduced. This was the straw that broke the camel's back.

4) People hid in forests or fought taxmen who arrived to collect 12 pence off everyone.

5) The rebellion was started off in Kent and Essex in June 1381, and was led by Wat Tyler.

### *The Main Events of the Rebellion*

June 1381 — rebels occupy London

14th June — Richard II meets rebels and agrees to some demands. Some rebels go home. Some murder the Archbishop and stick his head on a spike.

15th June — Richard meets rebels again and agrees to most demands. Rebels go home.

July 1381 — Revolt is over. Wat Tyler is beheaded and other rebel leaders are hanged.

## *The King Stopped the Revolt*

1) King Richard II was still only 14 when the revolt was going on.

2) The rebels killed the Archbishop of Canterbury and burned the Savoy Palace.

3) Richard met the rebels and promised that all of their demands would be met.

4) But, as soon as most of the peasants had gone home, lots of the rebel leaders were hanged, and Wat Tyler was beheaded.

5) The Poll Tax was abandoned, but peasants were forced back under the control of the lords.

## *The peasants are revolting — they chew with their mouths open...*

This was a pretty important event. It shows us how the feudal system was falling apart after 300 years. It also shows that people DID get mad at the Church, and weren't afraid to show it. Well I mean, they killed the Archbishop of Canterbury. It sounds like they were pretty upset to me.

# The English Medieval Church

The Catholic Church had a <u>huge</u> impact on everyday life in Medieval England. The stuff on this page is dead important to know about, as it affects <u>everything</u> in this period of history.

## Christendom *was* Wherever *the* Catholic Church *was*

Medieval England was part of <u>Christendom</u> — all the countries where most people were Christian. Under Christendom, <u>politics and society</u> were closely linked to the <u>Church</u>.

1) Christendom covered the <u>whole of Europe</u>, apart from bits of Scandinavia and some Muslim areas in Spain and southern Italy.
2) This meant that the beliefs and teachings of the Catholic Church <u>controlled</u> the way most people <u>behaved</u> throughout Europe.
3) Nearly everyone would have had some <u>link</u> with the church —
   - a family member might be a clergyman
   - they might pay rent to a church landlord
   - they might work for the Church
   - people had to pay annual tithes (taxes) to the church
4) People were <u>told they'd go to hell</u> if they didn't support the church.

> People left money to the church so that prayers could be said to shorten their time in purgatory. (Purgatory was where they'd go before heaven, to have their sins cleansed by fire).

Serves me right for supporting Oldham Athletic...

## The Church *was* Very Powerful

*Not everyone thought the Church was great. The Lollards (an English religious group) attacked the Roman Church's wealth and privileges. They were accused of being heretics. Many were burnt at the stake in the early 1400s. Nice.*

1) For most of the medieval period, the <u>Church was richer</u> than the King was.
2) The clergy <u>didn't have to pay taxes</u>, and ordinary people had to pay them for baptisms, weddings and funerals. People were told that they'd go to hell if they didn't cough up the money.
3) The Church could afford to build impressive <u>stone</u> churches and cathedrals. These could be used for defence, and have <u>lasted</u> for centuries (most other buildings were just built of wood).
4) Bishops became <u>political figures</u>. Some of them <u>controlled</u> important areas of England (like bits near the Scottish border).

## Parish Priests *Were Expected to* Do Loads

The Church had an <u>organised structure</u>. The <u>Pope in Rome</u> was at the head, and had a network of bishops and senior clergy to help him maintain power. At the bottom was the <u>parish priest</u>.

That'll be £17,000 please

1) Priests told the villagers what to do and how to <u>behave</u>.
2) Priests were <u>not</u> normally of <u>noble birth</u>.
3) They <u>weren't</u> supposed to get <u>married</u> (though some did).
4) They earned an income from <u>farming</u> done on the church lands (called the glebe).
5) They took services, said mass and heard confession.
6) They were expected to <u>teach</u> local children, and <u>help</u> out the sick and the poor.

Some priests were <u>good</u> — they cared for their parishes and tried to help the poor.
Some priests were <u>bad</u> — greedy, lazy, not very well educated, caring more about money, women and pleasure than they did about the Church.

## I've been to hell — they were serving luncheon meat...

Back in the middle ages, religion had a big effect on people's everyday lives. It wasn't easy to rebel either — you'd be threatened with hell and purgatory. Which don't sound like very nice places.

# Monks and Monasteries

LOADS of people used to go off and become nuns and monks. It was seen as the most sacred thing you could do with your life. And I'm not talking about a Sound of Music sing-along.

## Monastic Life has a Long History in Britain

Before the Romans came here, most of the population were pagans, and worshipped their own gods.

1) By the early 300s there were already some Bishops about in Lincoln, London and York.
2) In 400, St Ninan set up a monastery at Whithorn in Scotland.
3) The Romans left in about 410 and after that Christianity was only really popular in Wales.
4) Then in 597, a missionary called St Augustine landed in Kent. He was the first Archbishop of Canterbury and set up monasteries which followed the 'Benedictine Rule' — i.e. rules St Benedict made for a holy life. Most Medieval monasteries after this followed the Benedictine Rule.
5) Another important monastery was set up by St Columba and St Aidan at Lindisfarne in 635.

> *St Benedict had a vision of people living and working together in prayer, isolated from the outside world.*

## There were Lots of Different Monastic Orders

1) Cluniacs came from the Benedictine abbey at Cluny, in France, bringing a really strict form of Benedictine Rule with them.
2) Even stricter were the Cistercians, who were also from France.
3) The Gilbertines were different because they started in England. They had monks and nuns at the same monastery.
4) Carthusians came from France. They were a very strict order who fasted and took vows of silence.

> *Monks were great builders. Fountains Abbey in Yorkshire and Furness Abbey in Cumbria are just a few of the pretty amazing ruins that have survived and are open to visitors.*

5) Boys as young as 7 could become monks. Most newcomers joined when they were a bit older though. Vows would be taken at 16 — Chastity (no wives or girlfriends)
Obedience (obey all church orders)
Stability (never leave the monastery)
Poverty (never own nowt)
6) Monks had to go and pray at loads of different times — starting at 2am and ending at 8pm when they went to bed.

## Abbeys Earned Extra Money from Pilgrims

1) Many abbeys claimed to own a religious relic such as the bone of a saint or a splinter from Christ's cross. People made pilgrimages to look at them.
2) Pilgrims were also attracted to the tombs of saintly people, such as Thomas à Becket (see p5).
3) Pilgrims liked to collect badges and other souvenirs from the shrines they had visited — all of which they had to pay for.
4) The first great work of English literature (i.e. written in English, not Latin) is based around a pilgrimage. It was 'The Canterbury Tales' by Geoffrey Chaucer — an account of a group of pilgrims travelling to the shrine of Thomas à Becket and telling each other stories along the way.

## He's a wonderful monk — hardly any bad Habits...

Of course, that's not really true. Monks were sometimes responsible for nuns getting pregnant. The Chicksands Abbey allowed men and women in the same monastery. I dare you to guess what happened *blah blah* pregnancy *blah blah blah* castration *blah blah* you get the picture.

# English Jews 1066-1290

Okay — Medieval England was part of Christendom. Everyone was expected to be a Christian and go to church and give money to the church. But not everyone did...

## There Was an Important Jewish Community in England

There had been an important Jewish community in England since the 1000s, and Jews had made a major contribution to English society all the way through the 1100s —
1) Jews provided finance for wars and trade by lending the money.
2) They played a vital role in maintaining the British treasury.
3) The Jewish community also brought many new skills and crafts into England.
4) Lots of people disliked them, probably because they were jealous and didn't like owing them money.

## The Catholic Church Said Usury was a Sin

1) In the Middle Ages, lending money for interest was called usury and was considered to be a sin.
2) Christians were forbidden to lend money. Jews were forbidden to own land.
3) This meant that Jews became the money-lenders and were able to set high interest rates.
4) The people who borrowed money from them weren't too chuffed about this.
5) The Crown watched over Jewish financiers and their property, and taxed them harshly.

## Many Jews Were Massacred in 1190

The early part of 1190 saw many incidents of anti-Semitic behaviour and attacks on Jewish people.

Anti-Semitism means prejudice and discrimination against Jewish people

1) The biggest tragedy occurred at Clifford's Tower in York, on 16th March 1190 (a Jewish feast day).
2) Richard Malebisse, a local landowner, whipped up anti-Jewish feelings in the city of York.
3) 150 members of the Jewish community in York gathered together for protection in the wooden structure known as Clifford's Tower.
4) Rather than face the mob that had gathered outside the Tower, many Jews took their own lives.
5) Those who surrendered were massacred by the waiting mob. All 150 Jews died.
6) The mob were partly motivated by their desire not to repay money they had borrowed from the Jewish community. After the massacre the mob moved on to the cathedral, York Minster, to destroy the records of their debts which were kept there.
7) Not all the Jews in York were killed. Some of the survivors paid for the Five Sisters window in the north transept of York Minster.

## All Jews Were Expelled From England in 1290

1) 1216-72 — The reign of Henry III. Henry III wasn't a very good king. Jewish bankers gave him much-needed loans and finance as he struggled to control his powerful barons.
2) 1275 — Edward I passed an Act of Parliament banning Jews from lending money at interest. The King had begun to borrow money from Italian bankers and so no longer felt that he needed to protect English Jews.
3) 1280s — As England struggled with war and financial difficulties, anti-Semitism continued to rise and Jews frequently found themselves being used as scapegoats when things went wrong.
4) 1287 — Edward I arrested and imprisoned 3,000 Jews and demanded ransoms for their release.
5) 1290 — Finally Edward issued an edict (command) that expelled all Jews from England.

## Clifford's Tower might be knocked down to build a car park...

People are protesting about it. That building (rebuilt in stone) marks an important moment in history that shouldn't be forgotten.

# *Revision Summary*

*Wow. Our history is pretty gory really. Lots of gruesome murders and things. Hmmm... I don't reckon I'd have liked it much back in medieval times. Well, there were no radiators for starters. That must have been a right pain. Plus the handkerchief only got invented some time in the late 1300s. That's an awfully long time to go without blowing your nose. People probably got a bit carried away with blowing their noses to start with. I guess they'd have had quite a lot of gunk stuffed up there that needed getting rid of. Well. Anyway. Enough of that. Time for the revision summary. I know it's not as exciting as talking about snot, but you'll need these facts and figures at your fingertips if you're going to get anywhere with history, so make sure you go through this revision summary so you know everything on it. Yay...*

1) What year was the Battle of Hastings? (Round of applause if you can remember what day.)
2) Who was crowned King of England after the Battle of Hastings?
3) Name two places that William Rufus conquered.
4) What are the suspicious circumstances surrounding William Rufus's death?
5) What was the Domesday Book and when was it written?
6) In your own words, explain what a "villein" was.
7) What were towns like at the time of the Domesday Book? (Try to sum them up in a sentence.)
8) Why did England get involved in Irish affairs in Henry II's reign?
9) Which of the following best sums up medieval relations between England and Scotland?
    a)      difficult and unsettled
    b)      kinda groovy
    c)      the great-aunt on his mother's side
10) Which king of England conquered Wales in the 1270s?
11) Name 3 battles which were won by the English over the Hundred Years War.
12) Who did Henry I decide should be his heir after the White Ship sank in 1120?
13) Explain in 3 sentences what actually happened after Henry I died.
14) What did Henry II do to make the court system better?
15) Who was Thomas à Becket, and why was he killed?
16) Name the two sons of Henry II who became kings.
17) Where and when was King John forced to sign the Magna Carta?
18) What were the three main issues dealt with by the Magna Carta.
19) Roughly what percentage of people in Britain died because of the Black Death?
20) Write a paragraph to explain how the Black Death actually made things better for the survivors.
21) What were "tithes", and who had to pay them?
22) What year was the Peasants' Revolt led by Wat Tyler?
23) What was King Richard II's role in the revolt?
24) Where was Christendom in the Middle Ages?
25) Which of the following is the correct definition of purgatory?
    a)      the place where people went after they died, in order to have their sins cleansed by fire.
    b)      history lessons.
26) Write a paragraph describing the role of a parish priest.
27) What were the four vows that were taken by monks?
28) What is meant by the term "usury"?
29) What is meant by the term "Anti-Semitism"?
30) Write a paragraph describing the Massacre at Clifford's Tower in 1190. You should describe the actual events, as well as suggesting why you think it happened.
31) When were all Jews expelled from England by Edward I?

# Religion in Tudor England

Religion was a hot political potato for the Tudor kings and queens. The big changes started when Henry VIII broke away from the Roman Catholic Church and put the English Church under his control.

## Religion **was** Important **because it was Linked to** Politics

*The Jesuit (Catholic) priest Edmund Campion was executed as a traitor during Elizabeth's reign.*

*Some extreme Protestants, called Puritans, wanted more reforms than Elizabeth was prepared to allow. John Stubbs had his hand cut off for printing a book that supported Puritanism.*

1) Today people are mostly free to worship however they want. In the 1500s it was different — religion was tied up with politics and there was very little religious tolerance.

2) Rulers wouldn't allow their subjects to follow other faiths. This was believed to be disloyal and subversive.

3) For example, Elizabeth I decided on a middle ground of very mild Protestantism and wanted all her subjects to follow it. People who continued to support other faiths were punished.

## Henry VIII **Broke** Away **from the** Roman Catholic **Church**

1) Henry VIII followed the Catholic Church at first and was called Defender of the Faith by the Pope. But his Catholic wife Catherine of Aragon didn't give him a son.

2) Henry decided he wanted to marry Anne Boleyn instead, but the Pope in Rome wouldn't let him get divorced.

3) Henry stayed Catholic, but he broke away from Rome and got rid of the monasteries because:
   - he wanted a son to follow him
   - he fancied Anne Boleyn
   - he was short of money
   - he wanted the extra power of controlling the Church
   - he could keep the nobles happy by giving them church lands

1532 — Henry stopped all payments going from the Church in England to Rome.

1533 — His marriage was annulled and he married Anne.

1534 — Henry made himself Head of the Church in England and the Act of Supremacy made this official.

1536 onwards — He attacked the Catholic monasteries and took their valuables and land.

1539 — Bible was translated into English. Act of Six Articles was passed which supported Catholicism.

*Catherine was the widow of Henry's elder brother Arthur. To get out of his marriage, Henry used a Bible extract that says you can't marry your brother's widow.*

## Problems **were** Caused **by Breaking Away from** Rome

1) Many Catholics still felt loyal to the Pope.
2) People resented the nobles getting the Church lands and wealth.
3) Catherine of Aragon was the aunt of Charles V — one of the most powerful rulers in Europe. Henry was creating a powerful enemy by annulling his marriage to Catherine.
4) When the monasteries were dissolved poor people lost a source of charity.
5) The dissolution of the monasteries provoked the Pilgrimage of Grace — a revolt of 40,000 people in the north of England.
6) The break away from Rome encouraged Protestants to quarrel more with the Catholic Church.

## The Pope is dead — long live the King...

Tudor religion is complicated. As a brief reminder — Henry VIII broke away from the Pope but was still Catholic. He just wanted to have control over the church and do whatever the heck he wanted.

# Religion in Tudor England

All the religious changes in England weren't happening in a vacuum —
there were major religious arguments and changes going on in <u>Europe</u> as well.

## The Reformation was Happening in Europe

1) In the 1500s people in <u>Northern Europe</u> started getting seriously annoyed with <u>corruption</u> and <u>superstition</u> in the Roman Catholic church.
2) Religious thinkers like <u>Martin Luther</u> (a German friar) and <u>John Calvin</u> (a French priest) wrote books and articles protesting about the state of the Catholic church.
3) Protestants like Calvin and Luther wanted to <u>reform</u> Christian religion and make it easier for <u>ordinary people</u> to understand — e.g. by <u>translating</u> the bible from Latin so ordinary people could understand it.
4) To the Catholic church, Protestants were <u>heretics</u>. Some were <u>executed</u>, though the famous ones like Luther and Calvin survived.

## Edward VI was fairly Protestant, but Mary was Catholic

Henry VIII died in 1547 and his 9-year old son <u>Edward</u> became King. Edward had been brought up by a <u>Protestant</u>. Most English people were still Catholics, but Edward supported Protestants by:

1) saying that priests could <u>marry</u> (Catholic priests couldn't)
2) introducing a new <u>Book of Common Prayer</u> in 1549, written in <u>English</u>
3) passing the <u>Act of Uniformity</u> to make everyone use the new Book of Common Prayer
4) making services <u>simpler</u> and churches <u>barer</u>, in the Protestant fashion

Edward died young in 1553. His sister <u>Mary</u> became queen and ruled until her death in 1558. She was a <u>strong Catholic</u> who tried to <u>reverse</u> the religious changes of the previous reigns.

*Burning cleanses the soul.*

**Mary, 1553-1558**

1) She got rid of the Prayer books and the Act of Uniformity.
2) She <u>restored</u> the rule of the <u>Pope</u> over the Church in England in 1554 and married the Catholic Philip II of Spain.
3) She had about <u>300 Protestants burnt</u> — including famous churchmen like Cranmer, Latimer, and Ridley. This led her to be labelled '<u>Bloody Mary</u>' by Protestants like John Foxe.

*We know about many of the people who died for their religion because of a book by John Foxe, called Foxe's Book of Martyrs.*

## Elizabeth I tried a Moderate Religious Policy

1) <u>Elizabeth I</u> (1558-1603) tried to allow both Catholics and Protestants to worship — all under the official structure of the <u>Church of England</u>. As long as people went to church she didn't ask too much about what they believed.

2) She called herself <u>Governor</u> of the Church of England, rather than Head, by an <u>Act of Supremacy</u> (1559). A new <u>Act of Uniformity</u> (1559) insisted that everybody used a new prayer book. It was worded in a way that wouldn't offend Catholics too much.

3) As time passed, there were <u>threats</u> to her life from Catholics and she became <u>harsher</u> in her treatment of them. <u>Catholics</u> found themselves having to worship in <u>secret</u>.

*The Puritans were extreme Protestants who thought hard work and worship were really important. They strongly opposed frivolous things like theatre, dancing and alcohol.*

## Forget burning Protestants — she drank tomato juice...

Bloody Mary was just averagely bloody by 1500s standards. All the Tudors executed lots of people.

# Mary Queen of Scots / The Armada

It's not nice when some of your biggest problems come from your own family.
Mary Queen of Scots was a real problem to Elizabeth, and they were cousins.

## Elizabeth had Mary Queen of Scots Executed

1) Mary Stuart, the daughter of James V of Scotland, married the French King. She returned to Scotland when her husband died.

2) By then, Protestant leaders like John Knox had become powerful in Scotland — and Mary was a Catholic. She married Lord Darnley, who was murdered in 1567, and then (foolishly) married the unpopular Earl of Bothwell.

3) She was forced to flee from Scotland to England, asking for Elizabeth's help. Her name was associated with several Catholic plots to kill Elizabeth, so Queen Liz imprisoned her. Eventually, Elizabeth agreed to have her executed, and Mary was beheaded.

1561 — Mary returns to Scotland as Queen.
1565 — Marries Lord Darnley. Has a son called James.
1567 — Darnley murdered. Mary marries Bothwell.
1568 — Flees to England. Kept under Elizabeth I's protection for 19 years.
1587 — Mary is executed.

## Relations between England and Spain got Worse

Philip II (King of Spain) got on well with Elizabeth to begin with, and even asked to marry her. But relations between the two countries gradually got worse.

1) Philip had been married to the English queen Bloody Mary, and he wanted his power in England back.
2) Many people in Catholic Spain thought that the Protestant Elizabeth should not be on the throne.
3) Elizabeth had been secretly encouraging attacks on Spanish ships.
4) Elizabeth had been quietly helping Spain's enemies in the Netherlands.
5) In 1587 she executed Mary Queen of Scots — a Catholic queen.
6) The Pope had written an open letter (papal bull) to all Catholics, saying that they shouldn't obey Elizabeth.

## The Spanish Armada was Defeated

In May 1588 Philip sent the Spanish Armada (a fleet of boats) against England. Within a few weeks what was left of the fleet was limping home, by escaping round the top of Britain and back past Ireland. It was a disaster because —

1) The leader of the Armada, Medina Sidonia, was a soldier rather than a sailor.
2) The English had faster ships and better sailors.
3) The Spanish soldiers who were supposed to meet up with the Armada couldn't get there.
4) The English had crippled the Spanish fleet while it was in Calais harbour by sending in fire-ships.
5) The Armada hadn't planned to sail all the way round Britain, but they were forced to escape. Ships were destroyed on rocks.

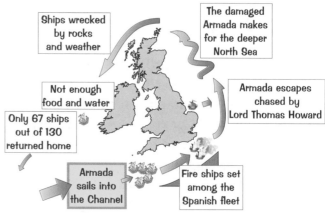

The damaged Armada makes for the deeper North Sea

Ships wrecked by rocks and weather

Not enough food and water

Only 67 ships out of 130 returned home

Armada escapes chased by Lord Thomas Howard

Armada sails into the Channel

Fire ships set among the Spanish fleet

## Elizabeth 2 — Catholics 0...

Mary Queen of Scots is very glamorous and loads of books and films have been done about her. Elizabeth is supposed to have been really angry when Mary was executed — she signed the death warrant but said she didn't mean to send it. Piffle. Terrible excuse. Anyway, one more page done...

# Elizabeth I — Marriage and Poverty

Elizabeth had some other big problems to deal with in her reign — who she should marry was a massive headache, and so was what to do with all those pesky poor people.

## The Question of Marriage and Succession was Important

Over twenty-six important men asked to marry Elizabeth I, and she said <u>no</u> to all of them. Elizabeth had to be careful about her <u>choice of husband</u> for lots of reasons.

1) She had to put <u>England first</u>, and not join with countries that many people hated, like Spain.

2) She didn't want to marry a foreign king if it meant a <u>foreigner gaining power</u> over England.

3) She had to be careful that her future husband's <u>religion</u> wouldn't cause trouble.

4) She didn't dare marry an English nobleman like Lord Dudley (who she really fancied) because that would make the other <u>nobles jealous</u>.

5) She was the last of Henry VIII's children alive and needed to have a child so there would be an <u>heir</u> to the throne. Otherwise people might <u>fight</u> over the throne after she died.

In the end, she stayed single, although she wasn't all that happy about it. Her councillors were worried about the <u>succession</u>, and kept trying to get her to marry.

## Poverty was a Big Problem in Elizabethan England

Elizabeth faced a growing problem with <u>poverty</u> in England.

1) The <u>monasteries</u> had been <u>dissolved</u> under Henry VIII — these had helped poor people in the past.
2) The <u>population</u> was <u>increasing</u>, so there were more people needing housing, food and jobs.
3) Rich landowners were <u>fencing off land</u> and this stopped many poor people being able to make a living on the <u>common land</u>.
4) <u>Sheep farming</u> was catching on, which takes a lot less workers than growing wheat.
5) Many poor people wandered to the <u>towns</u>, where there were <u>few jobs</u>.
   This led to more crime, as people tried to stay alive by <u>stealing</u> from others.

## Parliament Passed New Poor Laws

It was this <u>fear of crime</u> from wandering poor that made the government bring in <u>harsh laws</u>. They <u>divided poor people</u> up into:

<u>Sturdy beggars</u> — these were people who were thought to be skiving — they were made to live and work in workhouses.

<u>The deserving poor</u> — people who couldn't work through no fault of their own. They were given some money and could stay in their homes.

The Acts of 1597 and 1601 lasted for <u>over 200 years</u>. Although they didn't solve the problem properly, they were a start.

## Liz had a problem with poverty — but not her own...

Ah, what a beautiful, simple page. There's <u>two main things</u> to learn — why Elizabeth <u>couldn't marry</u> whoever she wanted (like that dishy Robert Dudley) and the problem of poverty during her reign.

# Portraits

Visual images have been used throughout history as a means of <u>propaganda</u>. Propaganda is the type of political communication (written or visual or spoken) that tries to tell you what to think.

## Portraits *Show What the* Sitter *Wants You to See*

1) In Tudor times most people (especially poor people) would never see the monarch in person — looking at <u>portraits</u> would have been the only way to know what the monarch looked like.
2) Therefore it was important for the <u>ruler</u> to have portraits that showed them in a <u>good light</u>. Portraits of rulers were often designed to show them as <u>powerful</u>, <u>attractive</u>, rich and wise.
3) Some of these kinds of characteristics were suggested with <u>symbolism</u>. For example, rich clothes and jewellery suggested the sitter was <u>wealthy</u> and a Bible or crucifix suggested they were <u>devout</u>.

## *There is a lot of* Symbolism *in Portraits of* Elizabeth I

<u>Portraits</u> of <u>Elizabeth I</u> use lots of symbolism e.g. 'The Rainbow Portrait', 'The Pelican Portrait', 'The Armada Portrait', 'The Ditchley Portrait', 'The Phoenix Portrait', 'The Sieve Portrait' and 'The Ermine Portrait.' These are some of the weirdest symbols used in them —

'The Rainbow Portrait'

Rainbow — symbol of peace, calm after storm
Eyes and ears — Elizabeth could see and hear everything
Snake — prudence
Ermine (little animal) — white fur a symbol of purity
Cherries — sweetness
Tudor Rose — Elizabeth had a right to the throne
Phoenix (mythical bird) — symbol of the Protestant Church
Rose with no thorns — symbol of Elizabeth's marriage to England
Feather fan — symbol of overseas power
Pelican — symbol of sacrifice for people and church
Fleur de lis — symbol of Elizabeth's claim to the French throne
Sieve — purity and innocence
Clothing, gloves, jewellery — power, elegance, sometimes purity

## *There are also* Hidden Codes *in Later Paintings*

This painting from the 1700s contains lots of symbolism.

'Mr and Mrs Robert Andrews' by Gainsborough, 1750

Land in the background — represents wealth and power
He holds a gun — He's prepared to defend his land and has a game licence to shoot
Corn in the fields — a symbol of fertility

But, this painting caused an uproar when it came out. The couple's clothes show they can't be rich enough to own the land they're on. Ooh, those cheeky lower-middle-class rascals...

## *The Good, the Bad and the Ugly...*

So make sure to be a bit <u>cynical</u> when looking at old portraits. Who paid for the picture to be painted? What was the purpose of the picture? What do the symbols in the picture mean? And remember paintings only show a small section of society — the rich and powerful, not the <u>poor</u>.

# The English Civil War — Overview

In the 1600s things got tense between <u>Crown</u> and <u>Parliament</u>. The main quarrels were over <u>power</u>, the relationship between the monarchy and Parliament, and the <u>religion</u> of England.

## Charles I (1625-49) made some Unpopular Decisions

1) Charles was responsible for <u>expensive wars</u> with France, Spain and Scotland. He also had to deal with rebellions in <u>Ireland</u>.

2) When Parliament refused to let him raise more taxes, Charles resorted to <u>illegal taxation</u> and tried to rule <u>without Parliament</u>.

3) Charles supported 'high church' ceremonies and some people worried he wanted to make England <u>Catholic again</u>.

4) He made enemies by asking for <u>Ship Money tax</u> — which was usually only collected when there was a war on.

5) Charles tried to do without Parliament for 11 years (1629-40). This finally led to <u>Civil War</u> in <u>1642</u> and led to <u>seven years</u> of struggle between <u>Royalists</u> and <u>Parliamentarians</u>.

I said I'M the king. Uh huh huh...

## Was Charles I a Successful Monarch?

Whether you think Charles was a <u>good monarch</u> depends on what you think a good king <u>should</u> be like, e.g.

- Stay out of <u>debt</u>
- Have good relations with <u>Parliament</u>
- Stay out of arguments about <u>religion</u>
- Be successful in <u>war</u>

Charles messed up in all these areas —
• He had money problems
• He wanted to limit Parliament's power
• He caused uncertainty about religion
• He was beaten in war by the Scots
Still, he was an old-fashioned monarch living in changing times. He thought he had a <u>divine right</u> to rule, with no need to share power with Parliament — just like in the old days.

## The Civil War was Fought From 1642 to 1648

*Parliamentarians called the Royalists '<u>Cavaliers</u>' after the Spanish word 'caballeros', which means armed horsemen.*

*Royalists called the Parliamentarians '<u>Roundheads</u>' because of the close-cropped heads of apprentices from London who supported Parliament.*

1641-2 — Conflict between King and Parliament over war and taxes.
1642-8 — Battles between Royalists and Parliamentarians.
1648 — Charles I defeated by Cromwell's New Model Army at Preston. England became known as "The Commonwealth", with Cromwell as President.
1649 — Charles I tried for treason and executed.
1651 — Cromwell crushes attempt to get throne by Charles I's son, <u>Charles II</u>.
1658 — Cromwell dies.
1660 — Monarchy restored. Charles II becomes the new King.

## Charles I — may have been a dictator but he had a nice wig...

Charles had a very rocky relationship with Parliament. They wanted more power — but Charles reckoned he was "<u>a little god</u>" with a divine right to rule, and he didn't want to share power.

# Causes of the English Civil War

Civil war was horrible. Some families ended up fighting each other, civilians who didn't want to be involved had fighting in their towns and soldiers raiding their property.

## There are Different Explanations of Why the War Started

### Religious Factors

1) Puritans wanted religious reform and were worried Charles had Catholic sympathies. He probably did — he tried to impose more elaborate services in church.

### Economic Factors

1) Charles was spending more money than he collected in taxes.
2) Illegal methods of taxation were introduced and old methods were revived.
   Overall, people were paying a lot more tax.

### Political Factors

1) Parliament wanted to have more power, but Charles didn't want it to.
2) Charles attempted to rule without Parliament throughout the 1630s.

### Social Factors

1) The population of England was growing quickly — contributing to poverty and unemployment.
2) There were tensions between social classes — the middle classes getting richer, the nobility declining.

## Some Historians Blame Long-Term Factors

Some traditional historians blame long-term factors for causing the Civil War —

1) Some historians say some of the problems went back to the reign of James I — he was unpopular with Parliament and they disagreed about religion and finance.
2) Class and other social tensions had been developing since the reign of Queen Elizabeth I.

What's up with you?

Apparently I'm a long-term cause of the Civil War.

Oh well. See you Tuesday...

## Other Historians Blame Short-Term Factors

A more recent, revisionist view of historians is that short-term factors were more to blame. These short-term factors are shown in the box below.

Build up to the Civil War
1630s — Proposed religious reforms anger Puritans.
1639 and 1640 — England was defeated by Scotland in the religious Bishops' Wars.
1640 — Charles called a Parliament in 1640. MPs began to demand political and religious reforms.
January 1642 — Charles tries to arrest five MPs by taking 400 soldiers into the House of Commons. They escape.
March 1642 — Rebellion in Ireland, but Parliament didn't want to let Charles have an army to crush the rebellion — it would give him lots of power.
June 1642 — Parliament pass the 19 Propositions that demand an increase in Parliament's power. Charles is angry and both sides raise armies.

## You're getting carried away Charles — don't lose your head...

Historians criticise older historians' work and come up with new theories. So when you study a historical event there's usually a traditional view and a revisionist view about what happened.

# Events of the English Civil War

There were two phases to the Civil War — 1642-1646 and 1647-1649. By the second phase the Parliamentarians were starting to win — their New Model Army was really tough and disciplined.

## The Major Events in the Civil War

### 1642 to 1646

August 1642 — Charles raised an army in Nottingham, while Parliament raised its army in London.

October 1642 — Battle at Edgehill, but no clear result.

1643 — Many battles, including Newbury, but still no clear outcome.

June, July 1645 — Parliament used the New Model Army to win important victories at Naseby and Langport.

1646 — Charles fled to Scotland where he was captured and sold back to Parliament.

### 1647 to 1649

1) In 1647 Charles rejected a deal to give Parliament control of the army for 10 years and to allow freedom of worship. He escaped from prison and made a new deal with the Scots.

2) In the summer of 1648 Royalists had victories in the North but were defeated by Cromwell and the New Model Army at Preston.

3) In January 1649 the House of Commons set up a high court of justice and although Charles thought the court was illegal it found him guilty and sentenced him to death.

*Parliament's Charges Against Charles:*
- *'Wicked design' to create unlimited and tyrannical power*
- *Tried to overthrow the rights and liberties of the people*
- *Fought a traitorous war against Parliament and People*
- *Responsible for treasons, rapes, burnings, damage of war*

## The Civil War Divided Families

1) Parliamentarian support was strongest in the South and East. The main support for Parliament came from small farmers, merchants and townspeople.

2) Royalist support was strongest in the North, the West and in Wales. A greater majority of the nobility and the gentry supported the King rather than Parliament.

3) Religion was the most important factor deciding which side people took. Parliament could count on the support of English Puritans. Catholics and less radical Protestants supported Charles.

4) It wasn't unusual for families to be split in their support for King or Parliament.

## Charles had Friends, but Parliament had Money

Although the Royalists had good generals, brave troops and were skilled horsemen, Parliament won.

1) Parliament had skilled generals like Fairfax, and Cromwell.
2) It had the well organised, trained and disciplined New Model Army.
3) It had control of the Navy and was able to block French supplies to Charles.
4) It was able to use taxes to finance itself, while the King had to rely on friends and supporters.
5) Charles proved to be a poor leader and made bad tactical decisions.

## New Model Army — bet they never got a spaniel named after them...

Religion was really political in 1600s England — it influenced which side people fought on in the war.

# England After Civil War

King Charles had gone, but the <u>arguments</u> about what should replace him were only just beginning. The period between Charles I and Charles II is called the '<u>interregnum</u>' — the period between reigns.

## There were Different Ideas about How to Run the Country

The winners soon began to argue amongst themselves. <u>Different groups</u> had different ideas about how the country should be run.

1) <u>Republicans</u> were happy to see Parliament continue to rule. It wasn't a full Parliament though — MPs who supported the King and all of the House of Lords were excluded. It was called the <u>Rump Parliament</u>.

2) <u>Royalists</u> looked forward to the return of the <u>monarchy</u>, hopefully in the shape of <u>Charles II</u> who fled abroad after his defeat in 1651.

3) The <u>army</u>, especially the generals, wanted to keep the <u>power</u> and influence they had during the Civil Wars.

1648 — A republic known as the Commonwealth was set up. At first the Commonwealth was run by the 'Rump Parliament' and by an executive Council of State. Oliver Cromwell was President.

1651 — Charles I's son (Charles II) tried to regain the throne, but was crushed by Cromwell at the Battle of Worcester.

### Some Groups Wanted Social and Economic Equality

1) The <u>Levellers</u> were <u>Puritans</u>. They wanted to abolish the monarchy and the <u>privileges</u> of the nobles. When the Levellers tried to build support in the army, <u>Cromwell</u> moved quickly to <u>crush</u> them.

2) The <u>Diggers</u> were a religious and <u>social movement</u> who wanted to farm wastelands for poor people's benefit. When the Diggers planted on <u>common land</u> at St George's Hill in Surrey their efforts were quickly destroyed by a local mob.

## There was a Struggle for Power 1649-1653

1) <u>Cromwell</u> strengthened his position as President of the <u>Council of State</u> by crushing revolts in <u>Ireland</u> and <u>Scotland</u> and defeating Charles II.

2) The retaliation to the rebellions in Ireland was cruel and bloody. In the town of <u>Drogheda</u>, about 3,000 <u>Catholic</u> men, women and children were <u>killed</u> by the English army. After defeating the rebels, Cromwell gave large areas of <u>Irish territory</u> to <u>English landlords</u>.

3) After a clash with the <u>Rump Parliament</u>, Cromwell <u>dismissed</u> it in 1653.

4) A <u>Nominated Assembly</u> replaced the Rump Parliament. It passed 29 measures dealing with <u>legal</u> and <u>religious</u> issues.

5) <u>Moderates</u> felt the Assembly was too <u>radical</u>.

6) Moderates and the army produced an "<u>Instrument of Government</u>" that named <u>Cromwell</u> as <u>Protector</u> for life (King in all but name) in 1657.

7) <u>Tension</u> between <u>civilian politicians</u> and <u>army leaders</u> increased. MPs wanted less religious tolerance, fewer powers for the army and a strengthened Parliament.

## The Rump Parliament — funny enough on its own...

Maybe England wasn't ready for a republic and completely new form of government. No sooner had they whacked Charles than they were trying to make Cromwell as much like a king as possible.

# Cromwell and Charles II

Oliver Cromwell was a <u>puritan</u> MP — he was really religious and believed God supported all his actions. He became powerful as a Parliamentarian <u>general</u> and ended up leading the country as Lord Protector.

## Views of Cromwell — Was he a Protector or Dictator?

**Cromwell as Protector:**

1) <u>Religious tolerance</u> for Protestants was established.
2) <u>Jews</u> were allowed to return to England.
3) Important <u>naval reforms</u> were introduced.
4) He made good decisions when dealing with <u>foreign countries</u>.

**Cromwell as dictator:**

1) The Protectorate was basically Cromwell's <u>personal</u>, <u>Puritan rule</u>.
2) He <u>sacked Parliament</u> for criticising his religious policies.
3) <u>Taxes</u> were collected without Parliament's consent.
4) <u>Judges</u> who ruled against him were sacked.
5) In 1656 some <u>MPs</u> asked Cromwell to take the title King. Cromwell knew the <u>army</u> was against the title of King. He dismissed Parliament and got the army to collect taxes instead.
6) <u>Dissent</u> was <u>crushed</u>, often brutally e.g. in Ireland and Scotland.

**Cromwell's Life**

1599 — Born in Huntingdon
1616 — Cambridge University
1640 — Became an MP
1642-48 — Rose through ranks of Parliamentary Army
1649 — Supports trial and execution of King Charles
1653 — Becomes Lord Protector
1658 — Dies, 3rd September
1661 — Dug up and 'executed' by Royalists

## The Monarchy was Restored in 1660

Cromwell had said that his son should be the next <u>Lord Protector</u> — as if he was a king passing on power to his <u>heir</u>. After <u>Cromwell died</u>, his <u>son</u> Richard ruled briefly and unsuccessfully. Richard was a <u>farmer</u> and not that good at ruling. Meanwhile, Charles II was living in exile on the continent.

*When Cromwell died he was given a massive, expensive funeral in London. Soon after Charles II came to the throne Cromwell's body was dug up, hanged and his head was stuck on a pole.*

1) In April 1660 Charles made the 'Declaration of Breda', promising to rule with Parliament and not punish his enemies if he was made King.
2) English politicians invited Charles II to be king. The return of the monarchy is called the <u>Restoration</u>.
3) Those who had signed Charles I's <u>death warrant</u> were <u>executed</u> and strict <u>anti-Puritan</u> laws were passed — this broke the promises made at Breda.
4) <u>Anti-Catholic</u> laws were <u>abolished</u>, although Parliament forced the new King to accept an anti-Catholic act in 1673.

## How Much Changed because of the Civil Wars?

1) The <u>monarchy</u> was <u>restored</u> — England didn't stay a <u>republic</u> for long.
2) The <u>Protestant Anglican church</u> of the interregnum didn't survive the <u>restoration</u> of the monarchy.
3) Puritans <u>lost</u> many of their civil and political <u>rights</u> after the restoration.
4) The <u>Glorious Revolution</u> of 1688 (which settled the nature of the <u>relationship</u> between <u>Crown</u> and <u>Parliament</u>) might not have happened without the earlier experiences of Civil War and Protectorate.

## Dictator/Protector — tomàto/tomáto...

Imagine being Richard Cromwell. Your dad kills the King, becomes a bit of a dictator and then leaves you to rule after he's gone. All you want to do is look after the farm. It's a strange life.

# The Glorious Revolution

James II was King after Charles. His <u>Catholicism</u> caused loads of problems. Britain's first political party — called the 'Whigs' — couldn't stand him and wanted a Protestant monarch instead.

## The Catholic James II didn't have Everyone's Support

Charles II died in 1685 leaving no legitimate male children. That only left his Catholic brother <u>James</u> to follow him, as James II. James wanted to <u>restore</u> the <u>Catholic</u> religion. He gave Catholics <u>important jobs</u> and in 1688 his Declaration of Indulgence allowed Catholics to worship freely.

As a result —

1) <u>Parliament</u> split into two groups — <u>Whigs</u>, who didn't want James on the throne, and <u>Tories</u>, who didn't think it was their job to stop it.

2) <u>The Duke of Monmouth</u> (an illegitimate son of Charles II) decided to <u>rebel</u>. The rebellion failed and he was executed.

3) At first James had no kids so the Protestants reckoned they could put a Protestant on the throne after he died. But then James had a son.

4) Some people asked James's <u>Protestant</u> daughter <u>Mary</u> and her husband <u>William of Orange</u> to take the throne. William of Orange came from part of what we now call Holland.

> In 1688 Protestants spread the story that James II's baby wasn't his, but had been smuggled into the palace hidden in a bed-warmer. James Edward Stuart was known as the Warming Pan Baby.

## William of Orange became William III of England

1) William of Orange didn't want Mary to rule on her own, and in <u>1688</u> decided to sail to England to <u>take the throne</u>.

2) James lost his nerve and <u>escaped</u> to <u>France</u>, and the throne was offered to both William and Mary. William of Orange became <u>William III</u>.

3) There were still many <u>supporters</u> of James II living in Scotland, Ireland and France. James' supporters became known as <u>Jacobites</u>.

```
                    James I
                   1603-1625
          ┌────────────┴─────────────────┐
       Charles I                       Elizabeth
       1625-1649                       Sophia m.
   ┌───────┴────────┐              Ernest of Hanover
Charles II      James II                 │
1660-1685      1685-1688              George I
                                      1714-1727
 ┌──────────┬──────────────┬──────────┐
Mary m.        Anne      James Stuart
William of Orange 1702-1714 (Old Pretender)
1689-1702                        │
                         Charles Edward Stuart
                          (Young Pretender)
```

Family tree of the Stuarts and Hanoverians

## The Protestants called this the Glorious Revolution

1) When William became King, the Protestants called it the <u>Glorious Revolution</u>.

2) <u>Catholics</u> didn't agree. They thought that the throne had been <u>stolen</u> from James and that he still had a right to it.

3) <u>Parliament</u> made sure that the new monarchs would not become too powerful and William had to agree to the <u>Bill of Rights</u> in 1689. In 1701 the <u>Act of Settlement</u> made Parliament even stronger and said the British monarch could never be Catholic, or even marry a Catholic.

4) This was the start of a <u>new kind</u> of monarchy — even though the monarch still had a lot of power, the people in <u>Parliament</u> had <u>more</u>.

I'm rich, I'm smug, I'm happy

I need a haircut

William and Mary, 1688-1702

## The future's bright — the future's William of Orange...

You'll understand all this better if you study the <u>family tree</u> on this page. Spot the danger from the Catholic James Stuart waiting to take the throne. And a major problem for the Protestants is that William or Anne don't have <u>any children</u> to follow them. Crikey. Amazing. Oh, I'll shut up.

# Impact on Ireland and Scotland

The Glorious Revolution was pretty inglorious in Ireland and Scotland. Many people in these areas were Catholic and supported James II. William of Orange defeated them — and it was very <u>bloody</u>.

## The Impact of the Glorious Revolution on *Ireland*

1) After <u>James II</u> escaped to France he went to <u>Ireland</u> to raise an <u>army</u> amongst Irish <u>Catholics</u>. He had 7000 soldiers with him, given to him by the King of France.

2) Catholics in Ireland had been <u>treated well</u> under James's rule and therefore <u>supported</u> him in his fight to <u>win back his throne</u> from the Protestant William.

3) James was quite successful at first, but his army was then badly <u>beaten</u> by William's army at the <u>Battle of the Boyne</u> in 1690.

4) The <u>Treaty of Limerick</u> in <u>1691</u> allowed some religious freedom to Irish Catholics and gave back some of their land. However these promises were broken and Limerick became known as the "<u>City of the Broken Treaty</u>".

*Some Protestants in modern Ireland call themselves Orangemen and celebrate the anniversary of the Battle of the Boyne.*

1688 — James II escaped to France. William and Mary took the throne.
1689 — James's army in Ireland laid siege to the Protestant city of Londonderry.
1690 — William's army took Belfast and beat James's troops at the Battle of the Boyne in June 1690. James escaped to France and never came back.
1691 — The Catholics finally lost the city of Limerick and had to admit defeat. Many Catholics had to give up their lands to Protestants who had supported William.

60 %    40 %

Irish Land 1640

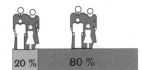

20 %    80 %

Irish Land 1689

 = Catholic occupied

 = Protestant occupied

Catholics lost ownership of a lot of land during the Glorious Revolution

## The Impact of the Glorious Revolution on *Scotland*

1) In Scotland, extreme <u>Protestants</u> called <u>Presbyterians</u> wanted the Glorious Revolution to go even further. Their Church system was called the <u>Kirk</u>.

2) <u>Catholic Highlanders</u> reacted differently — they supported the Catholic <u>James II</u> and were prepared to fight William of Orange.

3) At first things went <u>badly</u> for William in the <u>Highlands</u>. James's supporters, led by the 1st Viscount of Dundee, won the <u>Battle of Killiecrankie</u> in July 1689. But Dundee was <u>killed</u> at Killiecrankie and this weakened the Scottish forces.

4) The Highlanders were from different families (called <u>clans</u>) and there was some <u>infighting</u> — they <u>weren't</u> very well-organised or <u>unified</u>. William bribed some of the Scottish chiefs to stop fighting him.

5) Supporters of William <u>massacred</u> one whole clan, the MacDonalds, while they slept at <u>Glencoe</u>. The MacDonalds had refused to support William. William's <u>opponents</u> were able to <u>use</u> this terrible news to increase his <u>unpopularity</u> in the north of Scotland. Even after William won there were still lots of <u>Jacobites</u> left in Scotland who didn't want him to be King.

## Paths of Glory...

There's a lot of battles on this page. Sometimes you get the impression that fighting was all they did in those days. I can exclusively reveal that a lot of weaving and ploughing went on as well.

# England and Scotland United

In 1707 England joined with Scotland. The Scots weren't exactly thrilled but were bullied into it by England. There was a <u>Jacobite rebellion</u> against the English ruler in 1715 — but it failed.

## England Wanted to Keep a Protestant Ruler

1) Mary's sister <u>Anne</u> became queen in 1702. All of Anne's children died before she did. This was a big problem for <u>Protestants</u> who didn't want the <u>Catholic</u> James Edward <u>Stuart</u> (the Old Pretender) to claim the throne.

2) So when Anne died in 1714 the throne passed to a <u>Protestant</u> relation of Anne's who became <u>George I</u>. The royal family were called <u>Hanoverians</u>. George couldn't speak much English and spent a lot of time in Germany. He was not very popular.

*Hmm. Sausages.*

George I, 1714-1727

## The 1707 Act of Union United England and Scotland

<u>Uniting</u> Scotland and England was important for the <u>English government</u>. It would keep Scotland <u>under control</u> in case more trouble came from the <u>Catholics</u>. The Scots were forced to agree to union because the English <u>threatened</u> to stop <u>trade</u> between the two countries.
The <u>Act of Union</u> was passed in <u>1707</u>. These were its main points —

1) Scotland couldn't have its own <u>Parliament</u>, but could send 45 members to the English Parliament and 16 lords to the English House of Lords.
2) Scotland could keep its own <u>legal system</u>.
3) Scotland would have to agree to <u>Protestants</u> always being on the throne.
4) Both countries could <u>trade</u> equally.
5) Both countries would use the <u>same coins</u>.
6) Scotland would have its <u>own church</u>, called the Kirk.
7) Both countries would use the same <u>flag</u>.

*It was after this Act of Union that England, Scotland and Wales were referred to as "The United Kingdom of Great Britain."*

## The 1715 Rebellion against the Act of Union Failed

A lot of people in Scotland weren't keen on the Act of Union. They hated <u>paying taxes</u> to England and thought England was <u>interfering</u> too much in their way of life.
In <u>1715</u> <u>James Edward Stuart</u> finally made his move to take the throne. He and his supporters, the <u>Jacobites</u>, rebelled and invaded England. The rebellion was a failure. James's forces were <u>poorly led</u> by the Earl of Mar and both men ended up <u>escaping</u> to France.
The <u>Jacobites lost</u> because —

1) The <u>French</u> couldn't help because they were busy fighting elsewhere.
2) Many Scots were getting <u>richer</u> and didn't want to provoke harsh punishments.
3) Some Scots especially in the <u>lowlands</u> were getting used to English rule.
4) Some Scots didn't like James Edward Stuart's <u>links</u> with the French.
5) James had very <u>few supporters</u> in areas of the United Kingdom outside Scotland.
6) The <u>Jacobites</u> didn't always agree on what they wanted.
7) James <u>lacked confidence</u> that the rebellion would succeed.

## Moving swiftly on...

Phew. There's someone famous on the next page. After pages of boring nobodies, who wouldn't make it into 'Heat' magazine if they were around today, <u>finally</u> we have Bonnie Prince Charlie.

# Bonnie Prince Charlie

Next upon the throne after George I was his son George II. The <u>Jacobites</u> were still a threat, especially in the Highlands of Scotland. In 1745 Bonnie Prince Charlie started a new Jacobite rising.

## Bonnie Prince Charlie's 1745 Rising was Unsuccessful

By 1745 much of the British army was in Europe fighting — so the <u>Jacobites</u> took their chance. The <u>1745 Jacobite rising</u> was led by <u>Charles Edward Stuart</u>, who was the son of James Edward Stuart (the Old Pretender). Charles was known as the <u>Young</u> Pretender or <u>Bonnie Prince Charlie</u>.

### The 1745 Jacobite rising

1745 — Charles landed in Scotland. Thousands of Highlanders joined him. By the end of the year they had taken Edinburgh and captured Carlisle. They advanced into England as far as Derby, hoping to gather support. They realised that they weren't strong enough and retreated to Scotland.

1746 — English forces were being strengthened and were now led by the king's son, the cruel Duke of Cumberland. The Scots won the battle at Falkirk but many of Charles's army went home.

April 1746 — The Scottish forces were savagely defeated at Culloden. Charles escaped to France where he died in 1788.

*After the defeat at Culloden, Charlie was a wanted man, with a reward of £30,000 offered for his capture. A woman called Flora MacDonald dressed him as her serving woman and took him to the Isle of Skye — and from there he escaped to France.*

*"God save the King" became the new national anthem after Culloden, to celebrate the Hanoverian victory.*

The <u>defeat</u> of the rising <u>ended</u> the <u>Jacobite threat</u> to English power in Scotland. The main reasons for the defeat of the Jacobite forces were —

1) The Jacobites needed help from <u>France</u>, and it didn't arrive.
2) <u>Cumberland</u> had ten of the best battalions and some troops from Holland.
3) Charles got <u>no real support</u> from the <u>English</u> or the <u>Lowlands</u> of Scotland
4) Charles was not a good enough <u>military leader</u>.
5) Many English people did not want another <u>Catholic</u> king.

## How United was the United Kingdom?

1) <u>Wales</u> had already been joined to England in <u>1536</u> by Henry VIII. <u>Ireland</u> was controlled by Protestants. After the Act of Union in 1707 joining <u>Scotland</u> to England, Britain was <u>officially united</u>.

2) But some people didn't think so. <u>Catholics</u> in <u>Ireland</u> hated the Protestant rulers. In <u>Scotland</u>, Cumberland was so <u>cruel</u> after Culloden that there was <u>hatred</u> of English rule in the highlands.

3) On the other hand, some areas were learning to <u>accept</u> the new <u>United Kingdom</u> and many people in Scotland were becoming <u>richer</u> through <u>trade</u> with England.

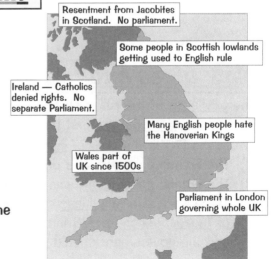

Resentment from Jacobites in Scotland. No parliament.

Some people in Scottish lowlands getting used to English rule

Ireland — Catholics denied rights. No separate Parliament.

Many English people hate the Hanoverian Kings

Wales part of UK since 1500s

Parliament in London governing whole UK

## Bonnie Prince Charlie — classic underdog material...

Bonnie Prince Charlie was a bit of a good-looking so-and-so, had a decent nickname, lost battles and dressed up as a woman. If you want to be remembered by history, this is the route to take.

# Causes of the French Revolution

A <u>revolution</u> is a time of sudden dramatic change and new ideas. One of the most famous began in France in 1789, when the people overturned a system that had lasted hundreds of years.

## French Society Privileged Some Groups Over Others

<u>French society</u> was organised into <u>three Estates</u>. The first two Estates (Church and Nobility) enjoyed great privileges. But most people belonged to the <u>Third Estate</u> which had no privileges and had to pay all the <u>taxes</u>. This system was called the <u>Ancien Régime</u>.

This <u>unfair system</u> was one of the <u>causes</u> of the <u>revolution</u>. During the revolution all the people that had privileges were <u>attacked</u>.

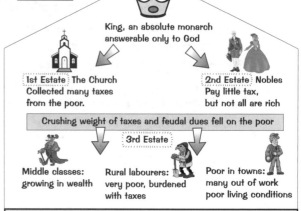

The Ancien Régime in France in the 1700s

**When the Revolution Came...**

- Church property was confiscated and sold.
- All noble titles were stopped and many nobles tried to escape abroad. Some of those who stayed were executed or imprisoned.
- Many clergy were massacred.
- The King was executed. France became a Republic — run by the people not by a monarchy.

## People had Different Reasons for Hating the Ancien Régime

What I wouldn't give for a domino's pizza...

1) Great events like this <u>aren't simple</u> to explain. It wasn't just about the <u>poor</u> rising up against the <u>rich</u>.
2) The poor in the <u>countryside</u> did not share the same problems as the poor in the <u>towns</u>.
3) The <u>nobles</u> had <u>grievances</u> against the King who had taken much of their power over the years and was now trying to tax them.
4) Some of the <u>middle-classes</u> had grown <u>rich</u>, but were <u>resentful</u> because they had <u>no rights</u> compared with the first two Estates.

## New Ideas and Economic Factors Were Also Causes

The <u>privileges</u> of the ruling classes aren't enough to explain why the Revolution happened. There were <u>other factors</u> that helped <u>cause</u> the revolution as well.

1) In the 1700s the <u>cost of living</u> was rising fast, but <u>wages</u> remained low.
2) The French <u>economy</u> was doing badly in the 1780s. There were <u>bad harvests</u> in 1787 and 1788.
3) The French <u>government</u> was getting heavily into <u>debt</u> — so it kept <u>increasing taxes</u>.
4) There were also <u>new ideas</u> spreading in the 1700s. For example the <u>American Declaration of Independence</u> in 1776 included such ideas as — people are born equal, people have rights and the government should govern in the interests of the people.

## Behind every good revolution — a bad harvest...

People need to be pretty fired up and angry about things to go to the effort of having a revolution. In the case of the French Revolution, there were shedloads of reasons why people were annoyed.

# The French Revolution

The National Assembly (see below) drew up the Declaration of the Rights of Man in 1789. It included similar ideas to the American Declaration of Independence — namely that people have equal rights.

## The Tennis Court Oath Triggered the Revolution

1) Some of the nobles and middle classes forced the King to call the Estates General in 1788. The Estates General was an assembly where representatives of the Three Estates could discuss matters with the King — it hadn't met since 1614.

2) However, the middle classes and nobles were disappointed by the Estates General and decided to form their own National Assembly. The members swore the Tennis Court Oath, saying that they would not disband until their demands for a new Constitution were met.

3) The new National Assembly was controlled by the middle classes. This gave hope to the poor in the towns and on July 14th 1789 they stormed and destroyed the Bastille — the King's hated prison in Paris.

The Storming of the Bastille
1) The Bastille was a hated prison and symbol of the old regime.
2) The storming itself wasn't very impressive — there were only 7 prisoners there.
3) Symbolically though the destruction of the Bastille was very important to the revolutionaries.

4) There had been peasant revolts since May. Throughout the summer of 1789 there were riots, and rich houses were attacked. This time became known as the Great Fear. Many rich people tried to escape from France.

5) In October 1789 a large crowd of women marched on the King's palace at Versailles. They brought Louis XVI and his family back to Paris. Most people still wanted a king, but one who was controlled by the laws of the people — a constitutional monarchy.

## Robespierre Oversaw The Terror

Attitudes to the King changed dramatically over the next few years. In 1789 many people still wanted a monarchy — but in 1793 the King was executed.

### The King's Downfall

1791 — The King tried to escape to Austria. People stopped trusting him.

1792 — France declared war on Austria in 1792. Austria was harbouring escaped French nobles. Marie Antoinette, the King's wife, was Austrian.

August 1792 — The war went badly and caused economic problems in France. The King became more unpopular and was arrested.

September 1792 — France was declared a Republic. This meant it was ruled by the people, not by a monarchy. There were massacres of clergy and nobles being kept in prisons. The King was put on trial.

1793 — The King was executed.

1) France was now being ruled by a strict group called the Convention. Most of its members felt strongly that the King must die — they saw him as a threat.

2) The leader of the Convention was called Robespierre. He was very cruel and oversaw the Terror. The Terror was a violent period from 1793-94 when more than 12,000 people were guillotined.

3) Robespierre was turned on by his own supporters in 1794 — the Convention voted for his arrest and he was executed.

## They seek him here, they seek him there...

Robespierre tried to kill himself as he was arrested, but just shot himself in the jaw. They patched him up and cut off his head anyway. Lovely jubbly, anyway section finished — phew...

# Revision Summary

*Flippin' heck — what a lot of history. Polishing off Henry VIII in a page, whizzing on to the French Revolution via Bonnie Prince Charlie and some Orange guy. Oh dear. But it shouldn't be confusing, not if you work through these questions. That way you can get everything clear in your head and go back and look up any stuff you don't know.*

1) Is this true or false — "In the 1500s religion was separate from politics."
2) Give four reasons Henry VIII wanted to break away from the Roman Catholic Church.
3) Write down three problems created by the dissolution of the monasteries.
4) Why did Mary Tudor become known as 'Bloody Mary'?
5) Which of the following sentences describes Elizabeth I's religious policy?
   a)     A moderate policy — attempting to keep English Protestants and Catholics in one Church.
   b)     A harsh policy — three thousand and forty three turnips were hung, drawn and quartered.
   c)     An unrealistic policy — it tried to make Britons become Mormons like Donny Osmond.
6) What year was Mary Queen of Scots executed?
7) Give three reasons why relations between England and Spain got worse during Elizabeth I's reign.
8) Was the Spanish Armada's attack on England in 1588 a success for Spain?
9) Write down:
   a)     Four reasons it was very difficult for Elizabeth I to choose a husband.
   b)     One reason it was important for Elizabeth to marry.
10) Give two reasons why there was an increasing number of poor people in Elizabeth I's reign.
11) Describe the difference between "sturdy beggars" and "deserving poor."
12) What is propaganda?
13) What might expensive clothes and jewellery symbolise in a portrait?
14) Say which of the following Elizabeth I wanted to be portrayed as in portraits —
   a)     wealthy, pure, powerful
   b)     powerful, rich, a floozy
   c)     powerful, pure, a bit dim
15) Write down three reasons Charles was unpopular with parliament before the Civil War.
16) Describe four key events that happened in 1649.
17) What was the 'Rump Parliament'?
18) Briefly give one example for each of the following factors that helped cause the Civil War —
   a) political factors  b) social factors  c) religious factors  d) economic factors.
19) In what year was Charles I executed?
20) Who were the Diggers?
21) What was the name of the new republic created in the British Isles in 1648?
22) Write down four ways in which Cromwell acted like a dictator.
23) What was the Restoration?
24) Why did the Whigs dislike James II?
25) Was William of Orange Protestant or Catholic?
26) Write a paragraph to explain who the Jacobites were, and what problems they had with George I.
27) Who won the Battle of the Boyne in 1690?
28) Describe what happened at Glencoe in 1692.
29) Which year was the Act of Union between England and Scotland?
30) Give three reasons why the 1715 rebellion failed.
31) Who led the 1745 Jacobite rising?
32) Who won the Battle of Culloden?
33) Describe the *Ancien Régime* in France.
34) Why was the storming of the Bastille important to the revolutionaries?
35) Briefly describe what "The Terror" was.

# The Industrial Revolution

The 1700s and 1800s in Britain saw great changes in farming, transport and industry. This is called the Industrial Revolution. Parts of Britain were more quickly affected than others.

## The Industrial Changes were Massive

1) Between 1800 and 1850 the population of Britain doubled from 9 million to 18 million — the fastest growth ever.
2) The growth in population may have speeded up the Industrial Revolution because it created more workers and consumers.
3) The growth of railways definitely speeded up the Industrial Revolution.
4) The steam engine had been developed at the end of the 1700s by Boulton and Watt. Its use in transport and industry gradually changed Britain's way of life.
5) Over 2000 miles of rail had been laid by 1850, connecting London to most major centres in England.
6) This led to huge growth in industries like iron and coal. Goods could be moved around the country quickly and easily.

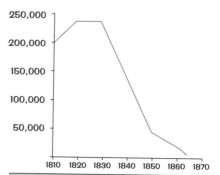

The number of handloom weavers working between 1810 and 1870. This shows that the lives of 1000s of people were affected by the introduction of machinery.

## The Rate of Change Was Different Around the Country

Different areas of the country were affected differently by the Industrial Revolution. The changes didn't take effect everywhere at once — some places still used older methods and machinery for a while.

1) It took quite a long time for many of the old crafts to die out. Some people were resistant to the new machinery and methods — they preferred to use their old methods and tools.
2) Some changes only affected some parts of the country. For example the steam engine in the textile industry affected workers mainly in the North and Midlands.
3) The changes were applied to some industries more quickly than others. For example, in 1850 there were still more sailing ships than steamships because they were better for long trips.

There appear to be a few leaves on the line...

Despite more changes, the average speed of a train in Britain today is still the same as it was in the 1800s.

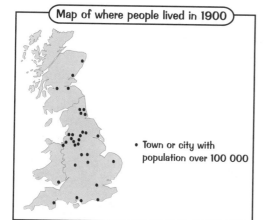

Map of where people lived in 1900

• Town or city with population over 100 000

## Some Cities Got Bigger

1) There were new factories and jobs because of the Industrial Revolution. Industrialised cities got bigger because people moved there in order to get work.
2) If you look at the map you can see that some areas of the country have more big towns and cities than others — some areas were more industrialised than others.
3) For example, the coal, iron, textile and ship-building industries were mostly based in the North of England and the Midlands. These areas had the most big cities. Agriculture was concentrated in the South.

## What did the Industrial Revolution ever do for us?

This bit of history's a bit dull, isn't it... Just smelly factories and dirty engines... Still, it was a revolution — it's pretty important. Take the steam engine... it meant people could get places much more quickly than by horse and carriage. They hadn't even dreamt of cars yet...

# Riots Against the Industrial Revolution

New machines and working methods were invented during the Industrial Revolution.
This affected the lives of ordinary people dramatically — and not all of them were happy about it.

## People Were Afraid of Losing Their Jobs

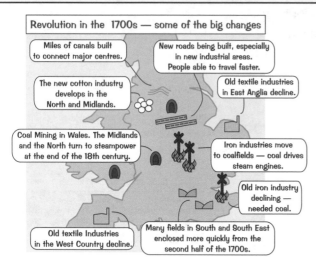

Revolution in the 1700s — some of the big changes

Miles of canals built to connect major centres.

New roads being built, especially in new industrial areas. People able to travel faster.

The new cotton industry develops in the North and Midlands.

Old textile industries in East Anglia decline.

Coal Mining in Wales. The Midlands and the North turn to steampower at the end of the 18th century.

Iron industries move to coalfields — coal drives steam engines.

Old iron industry declining — needed coal.

Old textile Industries in the West Country decline.

Many fields in South and South East enclosed more quickly from the second half of the 1700s.

1) Common land was being enclosed (fenced off). This meant many country people couldn't make a living because they had nowhere to graze their animals.
2) New machinery was being introduced in farming and industry, and many feared for their jobs.
3) Improvements in transport (especially roads and canals) meant industrial changes could happen more quickly.
4) In 1815 thousands of soldiers and sailors came home after the French Wars and found no jobs.
5) The price of wheat was very high, but wages were very low. So people couldn't afford much food. Britain saw the outbreak of several riots.

## Different Groups Started Riots

1) The Luddites were named after Ned Ludd (a made up name for their leader — they were too scared of punishment to use their real names). From 1811 to 1813 they smashed factory machines in the Midlands and the North.
2) The Swing Riots happened in 1830, when farm labourers attacked farm houses and machinery, demanding better wages and more jobs. They especially hated the new threshing machines that did the work of several men.
3) The Rebecca Riots started in the late 1830s — the rioters protested against high tolls (the charges for using the new roads). Their leader wore women's clothes in order to disguise himself.

*Some people say that the leader in the Rebecca Riots had been given clothes by a lady called Rebecca. Others say that it refers to a passage about Rebecca in the Bible. Either way, it makes for a good random picture...*

## Rioters were Executed or Deported

1) The Government came down harshly on all the people involved in these riots.
2) They executed many of them, or transported them to Australia as convicts.
3) A law of 1812 carried the death penalty for those breaking machinery.
4) Poor people who lost their jobs often had no way to survive other than by turning to crime.

The Government acted like this because —

1) they worried something like the French revolution might happen here (less privileged sections of society overthrowing the government)
2) they thought the poor had no right to say what should happen
3) many of them were landowners who wanted these changes to happen

Oh yes. This is much worse than farming in Cumbria. *heh heh*

## Stick some shrimps on the barbie — if Ken doesn't mind...

The government didn't feel much responsibility for helping people who were poor, unemployed and desperate. They saw labourers who rioted against change as trouble-makers who had to be punished. Still, being deported to Australia'd be OK — sun, surfing, barbecues...

# The Victorian Middle Classes

The Victorians believed in a class system. The upper classes were rich enough not to have to work. The working class had the worst, badly paid jobs. And the middle class was growing all the time...

## The Middle Class Grew During the 1800s

The middle classes grew during the 1800s. This was due to a number of factors —

1) The Industrial Revolution and the growth of the British Empire had a positive effect on Britain's economy. In the 1800s it was a wealthy nation, which could sustain a middle class of professionals, bankers, shopkeepers and merchants.

2) The Industrial Revolution meant that cities were growing and new cities being established. The British population was also increasing rapidly. People worked in a greater range of jobs with a greater range of incomes.

3) The growth of the railways, banking system and civil service led to an increase in middle class professionals running the administration. There was also a growth in other professions such as law and medicine.

## The Victorian Middle Classes had New Leisure Activities

1) With the railways came the possibility of day or weekend trips to the seaside. Resorts such as Brighton became popular.

2) Spa towns such as Bath and Buxton also grew in popularity. Victorians would go there to "take the water" for their health.

3) The Victorians enjoyed the theatre and music hall very much. Music hall was a bit like a variety show of singers, comedians and other performers.

4) The Victorian middle classes also loved sport. Many national games were developed at this time, for example rugby and cricket. The great cricketing hero of the day was W. G. Grace.

*Victorian bathers were very modest — costumes were bulky and covered all.*

### Middle Class Values
*The Victorian middle classes praised the values of thrift (saving), self-reliance and personal achievement. Many were attracted to groups such as the Methodists who preached against drinking alcohol and gambling. Perhaps as a result the Victorians have a reputation for austerity and prudishness.*

### Victorian Sporting Timeline
1823 — The first game of Rugby alleged to have taken place at Rugby school.
1866 — The Amateur Athletic club formed.
1871 — Rugby Football Union founded
1877 — The first official cricket test match.

## There was an Increase in Civic Pride

1) Cities were growing fast during the 1800s. In 1700 20% of the population lived in cities — by 1850 it was 55%. At first some of these cities weren't very nice places to live — they had grown too fast to have many public services.

2) There was an increase in civic pride in the late 1800s — people felt proud of the towns and cities they lived in. Wealthier Victorians spent money on the foundation of public parks, libraries, swimming baths and town halls.

3) There were also major Victorian building projects like the new Houses of Parliament in 1872 and the beginning of the London underground railway in 1863.

## Put that worker down Marjorie — you don't know where he's been...
Don't you just love the Victorian middle classes? They play cricket and enjoy theatre and have tea on the lawn while twirling dashing moustaches. It's what British people are like in Hollywood films.

# The British Empire — Overview

By 1900 the British Empire controlled nearly a quarter of the world. Britain began building its empire in Elizabethan times and it continued to expand until the 1900s through trade, wars and exploration.

## The British Empire Expanded from the 1600s to the 1900s

### The Expansion of the Empire

1600 — East India Company created. At first it just traded with India, then it started to set up outposts and settlements.

1607 — settlement of Virginia. Network of colonies in the West Indies. Colonised Barbados in 1625.

1700s — the British were the biggest slave traders in the world, and benefited from slave colonies, e.g. in Jamaica.

1763 — Treaty of Paris — Britain gains huge colonies e.g. Canada, Senegal, Florida.

1770 — Captain Cook claims New South Wales in Australia.

1775 — Lose thirteen American colonies in the War of Independence.

1793-1815 — Gain colonies in wars with France.

1870-1900 — The Scramble for Africa

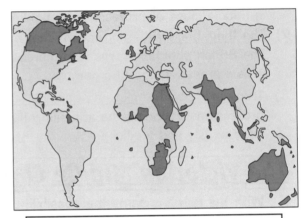

A map of the British Empire in 1915

1) During the 1600s and 1700s the expansion of the British Empire was motivated by trade. The idea was to gain as much foreign land as possible because this would be good economically — as a source of raw materials and labour and as a market to export British goods to.

2) During the 1800s Britain continued to gain territory and trading rights. The British PM Benjamin Disraeli (1804-1881) wanted to expand the Empire. He persuaded the government to buy shares in the Suez Canal which provided a trade route to India and the Far East.

3) Nationalist movements developed in many colonised countries during the 1800s and 1900s. They wanted independence from Britain. After the First World War the British Empire became less powerful and began to fall apart.

## The British Were Proud of the Empire

1) The Victorians were proud of their achievements and the power of the Empire and were keen to celebrate it.

2) Empire Day (Queen Victoria's birthday, May 4th) became a public holiday in Britain in 1902. Children were encouraged to dress up and sing patriotic songs. The last Empire Day to be celebrated was in 1958.

3) Many British people in the 1800s believed the British Empire benefited the colonies because they could have British government, Christianity and education.

4) Many people today would disagree with this attitude — but you've got to remember that at the time, back in the 1800s, colonialism was seen as a good thing by the majority of Britons.

Trading links with the British Empire meant that Britons could buy goods from around the world. This display of fruit, in a Cheshire shop in the early 1900s, includes dates and bananas.

## The Empire Strikes Back...

The British Empire is a pretty controversial topic. Some people today think that the British Empire and other European powers exploited the resources and people of the colonies unfairly (see p.47).

# Trade and Empire — India

Britain's interest in India started with <u>trade</u>. In the 1600s companies from England, Portugal and France set up <u>trading posts</u> along the Indian coast. The British increased their power in India and started to colonise parts of it in the 1700s.

## The East India Company Changed from Trader to Ruler

1) The <u>East India Company</u> was a <u>British trading company</u> that set up trading outposts in India from the 1600s.

2) The Company became <u>political</u>, and used a <u>private army</u> to gain land in India.

3) Robert Clive, a Company official, led an army that beat the French in a <u>battle at Plassey</u> in <u>1757</u> making Britain the biggest power in India.

1600 — Queen Elizabeth I signs the papers that set up a group of merchants with the name 'The East India Company'.
1608 — The Company first arrives in India.
1611 — The Company establishes its first factory and starts to make the transformation from a trading company to a ruling enterprise.

The East India Company had three main <u>bases</u> in India — Bombay, Madras and Calcutta. These were known as '<u>The Presidencies</u>', each having a <u>governor</u> in charge of local affairs.

1) <u>Madras</u> was founded in <u>1639</u> by the East India Company, and a fort was built there called <u>Fort St. George</u>. The <u>Bombay area</u> was given to Charles II as part of his Portuguese wife's dowry. He leased it to the Company in the 1660s.

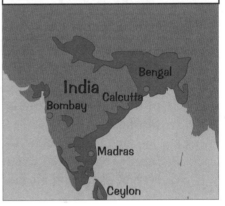

A map of India showing areas under British control in 1805

2) There was a <u>mutiny</u> in <u>1857-1859</u> of the <u>Indian soldiers</u> (called Sepoys) in the East India Company's army. They were <u>angry</u> because they felt British rule didn't respect <u>Indian culture</u> and traditions. They refused to use new <u>gun cartridges</u> which were rumoured to be greased with cow and pig fat (cows are sacred to Hindus, pigs are unclean to Muslims.)

3) They <u>killed</u> some of their <u>officers</u> and the <u>rebellion quickly spread</u>. It was crushed by the British and as a result the <u>Act for the Better Government of India</u> was passed in 1858. The <u>British government</u> took over the governing of India and also took over the Company's <u>army</u>.

## India was the "Jewel in the Crown" of the British Empire

1) <u>Economic control</u> of India was a massive advantage to England during the Industrial Revolution of the 1800s. Indians had to pay <u>taxes</u> to the British. India was used as a <u>market</u> which British goods could be sold to. <u>Products</u> such as indigo (a dye), <u>tea</u> and <u>cotton</u> were produced cheaply in India for the British market.

2) The Prime Minister Benjamin Disraeli bought shares in the <u>Suez Canal</u>, which opened in 1869, and provided a trade route to India. He persuaded Queen Victoria to be crowned <u>Empress of India</u> in 1876. India was viewed as the "<u>Jewel in the Crown</u>" of the British Empire.

### The Black Hole of Calcutta
In 1756 Siraj, the Khan of Bengal, asked the East India Company to stop fortifying settlements. They refused. Siraj attacked Calcutta and captured the fort. The British claim that the Indians then shut up a large number of Europeans in a small airless room and that many were suffocated. Indian historians claim only a small number of Europeans were imprisoned and those that died, died of previous injuries.

## The Brits would do anything for a nice cup of tea...

The Black Hole of Calcutta is pretty infamous. It's a nasty piece of history and no one can agree on what really happened. It's stuff like this that gives me nightmares...

# Explorers and Adventurers

Explorers and adventurers helped to expand the British Empire. They travelled to places the Europeans hadn't known about before — and many of these were then colonised. Not nice.

## David Livingstone was a Famous British Explorer

1) David Livingstone was born in Lanarkshire, Scotland in 1813. He worked in a cotton mill between the ages of 10 and 24. He then decided he wanted to be a missionary, and went to London to train as a doctor.
2) After spending some time in Southern Africa he travelled north into areas unexplored by Europeans and discovered new trade routes. He preached Christianity on his travels.
3) He found Lake Ngami, travelled up the Zambezi River and was the first European to see Victoria Falls (named after Queen Victoria). He travelled back to London as a hero. In 1866 he set off to find the source of the River Nile. He disappeared and was feared dead.
4) A New York newspaper sent the journalist Henry Morton Stanley (1841-1904) to search for him.
5) In 1871 Stanley discovered Livingstone at Ujiji, and greeted him with the famous words, "Dr Livingstone, I presume."
6) Dr Livingstone died in 1873 still searching for the source of the Nile.

### Other Famous Explorers and Colonisers

James Cook (1728-1779) — was a British sailor who travelled to Tahiti, New Zealand, Australia and Antarctica during the 1700s.

Mungo Park (1771-1806) — was a Scottish explorer who searched for the source of the River Niger. He wrote up his travels in the book "Travels in the Interior of Africa."

Cecil Rhodes (1853-1902) — made a fortune in African diamond and gold mines. Became Premier of Cape Colony in 1890. Bought rights to develop Matabeleland and Mashonaland and made them into the colony of Rhodesia.

Henry Stanley

## The Scramble for Africa was a Rush to Claim Colonies

In 1870 most of Africa was still independent. But from 1870-1900 there was competition between European powers to claim parts of Africa as colonies. This is called the "Scramble for Africa". It happened because —

1) There was competition for the resources of African countries, e.g. raw materials, gold, diamonds.
2) The Industrial Revolution in Europe motivated countries to claim new markets to sell goods to.
3) During the late 1800s there was a lot of rivalry between the European powers e.g. England, Italy, Germany, Spain, France and Belgium. The competition for colonies was part of this rivalry.
4) Some colonies had strategic importance e.g. South Africa was a good stopping point on the way to Australia.

### The Scramble for Africa

1870s — French expanded trade and influence in West Africa. King Leopold of Belgium tried to establish Congo Free State in central Africa.

1881 — Tunisia became a French Protectorate.

1882 — Egypt occupied by the British.

1884 — At the Berlin Conference the European powers discussed how to avoid partitioning Africa so everyone could have access — the talks failed.

1885 — Germany colonised parts of East Africa.

1890s — British colonised Uganda and Rhodesia. Italians penetrated into Somalia and Ethiopia.

## James Cook and Cecil Rhodes — discovered the Cookery Channel...

Well maybe not. Wonder if Cecil is related to Gary Rhodes? Nice pancakes. Shame about the hair...

# Wars and Missionaries

Wars also helped the British Empire get bigger — if they won a war against another European power they might gain a colony as a "prize". As for missionaries, they were very brave but a bit misguided.

## Missionary Activity had Positive and Negative Effects

1) There weren't many Christians in Africa at the beginning of the 1800s, apart from in Ethiopia.

2) Missionaries went to Africa in the 1800s to try and convert Africans to Christianity. There were both Protestant and Catholic missionaries.

3) The effect missionaries had varied. Some respected the African people — e.g. the Scottish missionary Mary Slessor, who lived in Southern Nigeria for over 40 years and learnt the local language. They sometimes brought knowledge about medicine or education with them.

4) Other missionaries were less admirable e.g. Friar Antonio Barroso persuaded the King of the Congo to sign a note, which the King didn't realise was an oath of loyalty to the Portuguese King.

5) Even though the missionaries were often well-meaning and worked hard, the effect of their work wasn't necessarily positive. They were purposely trying to change African religion and culture, and believed that European religion and culture were superior.

## Britain Gained and Lost Colonies Through War

There are three big examples of Britain gaining and losing colonies through war —

### 1. The Treaty of Paris 1763 — Britain gains Canada and islands in the West Indies

1) France and Britain fought each other from 1754-1763 to gain control of the New World. Britain won.

2) In 1763 they signed the Treaty of Paris which meant France had to give Canada to the British. Britain also got the colonies of Senegal, Florida, Louisiana east of the Mississippi plus the islands of Tobago, Dominica, St Vincent and the Grenadines.

3) This was on top of gains from a recent war with Spain when Britain had won the colonies of Grenada, Martinique and St Lucia.

### 2. The American War of Independence — Britain Loses Thirteen Colonies

1) Britain had thirteen American colonies in the early 1700s. After the war with France ended in 1763 Britain decided to take a more active interest in its American colonies.

2) New reforms and taxes were introduced by the British in the 1760s and 1770s and these were very unpopular with the American colonists e.g. the 1765 Stamp Act and 1767 Townshend Acts. These taxes partly paid for British troops and officials in America.

3) The Tea Act in 1773 stirred up even more protest. It gave the British East India Company a good deal importing tea to America — undercutting other companies. American patriots dumped a shipment of the tea into the sea in protest — this is called the Boston Tea Party.

4) The Americans eventually revolted against the British. The War of Independence went on from 1775-1783 and the American colonists won. Britain recognised the colonies as an independent nation in 1783.

### 3. The Wars Between France and Britain 1793-1815

1789 — The French Revolution

1793 — French King executed. French declare war on Britain and Holland.

1805 — Battle of Trafalgar. Stopped invasion by Napoleon. Death of Nelson.

1815 — Britain won the Battle of Waterloo and became the dominant power in Europe.

1793-1815 — During these wars Britain took over French, Spanish and Dutch colonies in the Caribbean.

## Without Abba life has no meaning...

Waterloo, I was defeated you won the war. Ooh-hoo. Waterloo. Tra-la la la. Woa-ho...

# The Reform Act and the Chartists

The political situation in <u>1830</u> was <u>elitist</u> and corrupt — less than 2 % of the population had the right to vote. Eligibility to vote depended on property, gender and where you lived. <u>Open voting</u> (everyone knew what you had voted) meant voters were sometimes pressured or bribed.

## The <u>1832 Reform Bill</u> Made Changes to the Voting System

The <u>1832 Reform Bill</u> brought in these measures —

1) 56 <u>Rotten Boroughs</u> were abolished.

2) More parliamentary seats were given to growing <u>industrial cities</u>.

3) Tried to extend <u>voting rights</u> for <u>men</u>.

4) This meant <u>300,000 extra voters</u> — now about 3% of the population had the right to vote.

5) The <u>working class</u> gained little — but these <u>early changes</u> meant that further reform would probably be easier in the future.

1815 — End of wars with France. Corn laws passed which kept bread prices high.
1819 — Peterloo massacre — 13 people killed when cavalry charged a meeting in St Peter's fields in Manchester.
1831 — Riots after the Reform Bill failed to gain House of Lords approval.
1832 — Parliamentary reform bill
1838 — Chartist group formed

*<u>Rotten Boroughs</u> — these were small constituencies, with very few voters, which could nevertheless send two MPs to parliament (because they'd always been able to). For example, Old Sarum near Salisbury was an old fort — no one lived there, but it still had two MPs. There were 56 such boroughs in 1831.*

## The <u>Chartist Movement</u> Wanted More Reform

The <u>Chartist movement</u> formed in the 1830s. It wanted more reforms and worked out a 'People's Charter' for reform which contained <u>Six Points</u> they wanted to be made law —

1) a vote for <u>every adult male</u> over 21 — so poorer people could vote
2) a <u>secret ballot</u> — voters would be protected from pressure from candidates
3) <u>annual</u> parliaments
4) <u>no property qualifications</u> for MPs — so poorer people could become politicians
5) payment of <u>salary</u> for MPs — so you didn't have to be rich to become one
6) constituencies of <u>equal size</u> — so a large city would have more MPs than a small town

## The Chartist Movement Gained Support when there was Unemployment

The Chartist movement <u>gained support</u> at first because —

1) People were angry that so little had been done for the <u>working class</u> by the <u>1832 Reform Act</u>.
2) Working people were angry about the <u>1834 Poor Law Act</u> which brought in <u>workhouses</u>.
3) The 1830s and 1840s were a period of <u>economic depression</u> with widespread <u>unemployment</u>.
4) <u>Middle class</u> support saw Chartism as a way to gain further <u>reform</u> of parliament.
5) Three <u>petitions</u> were presented to parliament in 1839, 1842 and 1848.
6) There was also some <u>violent protest</u> e.g. the 1839 Newport riots and the 1842 Stoke riots.

The Chartist movement <u>eventually failed</u> because —

1) In the 1850s and 1860s the <u>economic situation</u> was <u>improving</u> — so there was less discontent.
2) The <u>leadership</u> of the movement was <u>divided</u> on whether to use violent or peaceful methods.

## The Chartist's Six Points — wake me when they're done...

The Chartist movement didn't try to get women the vote — it still had old-fashioned attitudes.

# Changes to the Franchise 1850-1900

Lots of tricky terms in these few pages. 'Franchise' and 'suffrage' both mean the <u>right to vote</u> — especially the right to vote in political elections. It took a while for women to get it...

## There were Two More <u>Reform Acts</u> in 1867 and 1884

Despite the failure of the Chartist movement, their <u>demands</u> were campaigned for again, from 1865, by the <u>Reform League</u>. With <u>rapid economic</u> and <u>social change</u> many people felt that parliament still didn't fairly represent the people. Two more <u>Reform Acts</u> were eventually passed —

### 1867 Reform Act

1) The vote was given to <u>all male householders</u> living in <u>urban</u> areas.
2) Most <u>ordinary working men</u> in the towns got the vote if they were over 21 and householders or lodgers paying more than £10 a year rent.
3) The number of voters <u>doubled</u> to about two million men.

### 1884 Reform Act

1) This Act extended the vote to working men in the <u>countryside</u>.
2) For the first time <u>all</u> of the United Kingdom was under the <u>same electoral system</u>.
3) <u>Local government</u> became more democratic. Elected town and county councils replaced many functions of Magistrates and Poor Law Unions.

## The <u>Status</u> of Women <u>Was Changing</u>

In some ways the <u>status of women improved</u> during 1850-1900 period —

1) <u>Custody of children</u> improved after the Caroline Norton case — in which a drunken husband was allowed to take children away from their mother.
2) There were wider <u>employment opportunities</u>. Nursing was now a respectable occupation, following the example of Florence Nightingale. Increasing numbers of women were gaining employment in clerical work, shopwork and the professions.
3) The <u>Married Women's Property Acts</u> of 1870 and 1882 improved married women's rights.
4) The <u>Co-operative Women's Guild</u> (1884) <u>campaigned</u> for women worker's rights, divorce reform and better schools and pensions.
5) By 1901 some women were allowed to <u>vote</u> in <u>local elections</u>.

In other ways <u>women's position</u> in society was still <u>really bad</u> in the 1850-1900 period —

1) Women's <u>legal status</u> was still limited.
2) Women's employment was still mainly <u>low paid</u>, and <u>conditions</u> for factory work were poor. Women who had no husband's or family's support were exploited.
3) <u>Contraception</u> was limited and primitive. Many women spent much of their adult life <u>pregnant</u> and giving birth — which was dangerous health-wise.
4) <u>Women's reform groups</u> were seen as a <u>threat</u>. Many articles were written against the 'New Women' and Women's Suffrage (voting rights).

## By 1900 there were still Inequalities

1) There was <u>widespread support</u> for a limited measure of <u>Women's Suffrage</u>.
2) The <u>electoral system</u> was still a long way off from a modern idea of 'democratic'.
3) Other political and social <u>issues</u> were often regarded as <u>more important</u> than Women's Suffrage.
4) The <u>Liberal Party</u> was the most likely to bring in Women's Suffrage. But some Liberals thought if rich women got the vote they would vote <u>Conservative</u> — so they weren't so keen.

## The Cooperative Women's Guild — they'd do anything...

A lot of men didn't have the vote either in the 1800s — it wasn't just women who were excluded.

# Women's Rights

Back in the early 1800s government was completely male-dominated. Women couldn't vote and a lot of laws treated women as second-class citizens. No wonder some women got really angry.

## Many Victorians thought Women should stay at Home

1) Women didn't get the <u>right to vote</u> in national elections in Britain until <u>1918-1928</u>.
2) In Victorian times women had far <u>fewer rights</u> than men. For example until 1882 married woman couldn't own property — everything they owned became their husband's property on marriage.
3) Most Victorians believed men and women should have very <u>different roles</u> in <u>society</u>.

<u>Men</u> could take responsibility and be involved in the <u>public sphere</u> of life —
• Business and finance
• Politics and government
• The law and trade

<u>Women</u> were viewed as the '<u>Angel of the house</u>', taking responsibility for the <u>private sphere</u> —
• Care of children
• Managing the household
• Cooking, washing, cleaning

### Whether Women Worked Depended on Class

1) <u>Poorer women</u> worked because their families needed the <u>extra income</u>. They had jobs in mills, mines, domestic service or at home. They were <u>paid less</u> than men.
2) <u>Middle class women</u> though would aim to <u>marry</u> and not have to work. Instead they would learn <u>female accomplishments</u> such as singing, playing the piano, sewing and managing the household. As the "angel of the house" they were supposed to be dutiful and obedient.

## Three Contrasting Campaigners for Women's Rights

### Josephine Butler 1828-1906

1) Josephine Butler came from a <u>rich family</u> but became increasingly angry about the way women (especially <u>poor, underprivileged women</u>) were treated by Victorian <u>society</u>.
2) In 1864, 1866 and 1869 the <u>Contagious Diseases Acts</u> were passed. Parliament was worried about the spread of <u>sexually-transmitted diseases</u> in the navy and armed forces. The Acts allowed policemen to <u>force</u> any woman they suspected of being a prostitute to have a <u>medical examination</u>. Josephine Butler thought this was <u>degrading</u> and sexist. She <u>campaigned</u> for 21 years until the Acts were repealed.
3) Her campaigning methods included letter-writing, making <u>speeches</u> and encouraging women to <u>resist</u>.

### Harriet Taylor 1807-1858

1) She wrote a series of <u>essays and articles</u> which set out clear ideas on improving the status of women and their rights. She did a lot of work with her second husband John Stuart Mill, but it wasn't credited to her.
2) She <u>suggested new laws</u> to protect women from violent husbands (1851).
3) A key book, '<u>The Subjugation of Women</u>' was completed after her death by her husband JS Mill and her daughter Helen. Her daughter later became active in the Women's Suffrage campaign and the Kensington Society (which produced the first petition requesting votes for Women).

### Emmeline Pankhurst 1858-1928

1) She helped form the <u>Women's Franchise League</u> in 1889, which pressed for women's rights.
2) In 1903 she founded the <u>Women's Social and Political Union</u> (WSPU) to gain more publicity for women's rights — its motto was "Deeds not Words".
3) Between 1908-13 she was imprisoned several times for <u>civil disobedience</u> (demonstrating, breaking up political meetings, stone throwing) and went on hunger strikes while in prison.
4) WSPU action suspended on outbreak of war and its efforts turned to a patriotic support and recruitment of women to help the war effort. She formed the <u>Women's Party</u> in 1917.

## Forget Germaine Greer — Pankhurst kicked Edwardian ass...

Taylor is an example of <u>peaceful protest</u> and Pankhurst is an example of more <u>violent methods</u>.

# Women and the Vote

Be grateful you live in the 21st century.  Back in the 1800s there were no votes for women, no washing machines, no TVs, no microwaves, no Alton Towers...  but an awful lot of housework.

## Many Victorians Argued Against Giving Women the Vote

Arguments against allowing women more rights included —
1) Women's work and responsibility is in the home.
2) Medical opinion on the differences between men and women e.g. men had bigger brains than women and were therefore cleverer, or that women were 'hormonally unstable'.
3) Women were the weaker sex and needed to be protected.
4) Women were more individualistic and would be unable to co-operate, e.g. in politics.
5) Women would allow their emotions to affect their decisions about law and politics.

## Some Famous Victorians Supported Women's Suffrage

1) John Stuart Mill was one of many influential writers arguing for improvements in women's rights and status.  He was the husband of Harriet Taylor (see page 38).
2) David Lloyd George was the leader of the Liberal Party.  He had some sympathy for women's suffrage but was strongly against the violent methods of the WSPU. He was elected Prime Minister in 1918 in the first general election in which some women were allowed to vote.

## Campaigners used Different Tactics to Gain Publicity

Suffragists used peaceful and constitutional means to campaign for women's suffrage —
1) letter writing
2) wrote articles and journals
3) producing petitions
4) holding public meetings
5) trying to gain the support of MP's

Suffragettes lost patience with peaceful tactics and used more provocative methods —
1) heckled and broke up political meetings
2) smashed windows by stone throwing
3) made personal attacks on MPs and their homes
4) went on hunger strike when imprisoned
5) sought publicity — for example by chaining themselves to railings

## The First World War Speeded up the Pace of Change

Things changed for women during the First World War (1914-1918) —
1) Took on many traditional male jobs — drivers, engineers etc.
2) Worked in the Women's Land Army — replacing farmworkers who had gone to fight.
3) Worked to produce weapons in munitions factories.
4) Were able to take on more responsibility and to act independently of men.

1910 onwards — a majority of MPs supported Women's Suffrage.  Many also wanted universal voting for men.

1914-1918 — First World War — women took on traditionally male jobs

1918 — Vote given to all men over 21 and women over 30 who are householders or the wives of householders.

1928 — Women given the vote on equal terms to men.

## The suffragettes — from prison to citizenship...

Some suffragettes were really committed to gaining publicity for the cause.  Emily Davison tried to attach a suffragette banner to the King's horse in the 1913 Derby — she was trampled to death.

# Divided Ireland

The conflict in Ireland between Unionists and Nationalists is old and violent.
Problems date back to the 1600s — and the violence and arguments are still ongoing.

## The Nationalists are Catholic, Unionists are Protestant

**Nationalists**
1) Supporters are mostly Catholic.
2) They want one United Ireland which is free from British rule.
3) They are also called Republicans.

**Unionists**
1) Supporters are mostly Protestant.
2) They want Northern Ireland kept separate from the Irish Republic and to remain part of Britain.
3) They are also called Loyalists.

## There are Historical Reasons for the Conflict

(By eck it's gorgeous)

1) Elizabeth I and James I gave Irish land to loyal Protestant supporters which had been taken from Catholic rebels — this was called plantation policy.
2) A Catholic rebellion in Portadown in 1649 resulted in the death of about 1200 Protestants.
3) Oliver Cromwell crushed a Catholic rebellion in 1649 killing thousands of civilians in Drogheda.
4) William of Orange, the Protestant King of England won the Battle of the Boyne in Ireland in 1650, against the Catholic army of the previous English King, James II.

1798 and 1803 — Catholic rebellions
1800 — Act of Union
1845-46 — Great famine in Ireland
1850s and 1860s — Irish Republican Brotherhood (IRB) carry out some terrorist activities.
1886, 1893 — 'Home Rule' bill for Ireland attempted in British parliament, but it failed.
1905 — IRB is revived. The Nationalist party Sinn Fein is formed.
1912 — Third Home Rule bill to become law in 1914. The Loyalist Ulster Volunteer Force take up arms.
1916 — Easter Rising fails, 14 of the leaders executed.
1918 — Sinn Fein win 73 seats at Westminster, but refuse them.
1920 — Ireland is partitioned. Irish Republican Army (IRA) commit violent acts in protest.

### Hatred of English Rule

Laws were passed in Ireland to restrict the freedom of Catholics — discrimination was used as a method of control. As a result there was growing hatred of English rule, dislike of the Protestant Church and arguments over land ownership.

1) There were over one million deaths and mass emigration during the Great Famine of 1845-46 — the English government was slow to provide help.
2) The Act of Union in 1800 abolished the status of Ireland as a separate kingdom. Irish MPs would now sit at Westminster.

### Partition was Agreed in 1920

Attempts to introduce a Home Rule bill acceptable to both Nationalists and Unionists failed —
1) Both sides began to organise and train armed brigades.
2) The Irish Question was put aside by British politicians during the First World War. The Irish Republican Brotherhood rebelled for four days in 1916 — this was called the Easter Rising.
3) Two Republican groups (The Irish Citizens Army and The Irish Volunteers) combined to form the Irish Republican Army (IRA) in 1919 and began their 'War of Independence'.
4) Partition happened in 1920 with separate elections for North and South. David Lloyd George, the British Prime Minister agreed the Anglo-Irish Treaty — which created an independent Ireland but left the Six Counties of Ulster with majority Protestant populations as part of the United Kingdom.

## Things can only get better...

The violence and conflict in Ireland has been going on for centuries — it's a depressing situation.

# Events in Ireland since the 1960s

The modern period has been marked by <u>continuing violence</u> — revenge attacks and outrages in Northern Ireland and a terrorist campaign in the United Kingdom.

## The Civil Rights Movement was for Rights for Catholics

This was born out of a <u>long period</u> of <u>discrimination</u> in Northern Ireland <u>against Catholics</u>. Examples of this discrimination include —

1) <u>Employment</u> — higher unemployment among Catholics in Northern Ireland
2) Poorer treatment in <u>housing</u> provision
3) <u>Police</u> hatred of Catholics
4) <u>Political restriction</u> of Catholics' voting powers and influence

### The Troubles

In 1968 the first civil rights march took place. This movement was seen as a threat by many Protestant groups — The Orange Order had been revived and the UVF (Ulster Volunteer Force) had been secretly re-established. Violence against civil rights marchers led to further street violence and rioting, and troops were sent in to restore order.

## Main Events in Ireland 1970s – 1990s

1971 — Internment (imprisonment without trial) introduced. Ulster Defence Association forms.
30 January 1972 — 'Bloody Sunday' 13 civilians shot dead on march against internment in Derry.
March 1972 — Northern Ireland Parliament suspended. Direct rule from Westminster.
1970s onwards — IRA campaign of violence in England, mainly London and Birmingham.
1973-4 — Sunningdale agreement on power sharing.
1976 — Women's Peace Movement established.
1981 — Republican hunger strikers in Maze prison are allowed to die.
1985 — Anglo-Irish agreement tries to improve cooperation between UK and Republic of Ireland.
1993 — Britain begins secret talks with the IRA.
1994 — IRA ceasefire in August, Loyalist ceasefire in October.
1996 — Manchester bombing in UK. Violence at a march in Portadown.
1997 — Another ceasefire — and peace talks with the Labour Government.
1998 — The Good Friday Agreement. Referendum (people's vote) on its terms.
   In the Six Counties 71 % say 'Yes', in the Republic of Ireland 94 % say 'Yes'.

## Is a Lasting Peace Possible in Ireland?

With such a long history of discrimination, violence and revenge it has been <u>difficult</u> to keep a <u>lasting peace</u>. Segregation (separation) of Protestant and Catholic communities, distrust and hatred has fed <u>extremism</u> on both sides. The agreement of 1998 included —

1) a <u>new government</u> for Northern Ireland at <u>Stormont</u>
2) many convicted <u>terrorists</u> would be <u>released</u>
3) a <u>closer relationship</u> between the Northern Irish government and the Irish Republic
4) '<u>de-commissioning</u>' (handover and destruction) of weapons and armaments by Paramilitary organizations

### Map Showing Partition

NORTHERN
IRELAND
Belfast

REPUBLIC
OF IRELAND
Dublin

Cork

## The Good Friday Agreement is a hope for peace...

It remains to be seen if in the 21ˢᵗ Century the <u>cycle of violence</u> has been broken for good. It would be good if it could. And so, on a rather downbeat note, the section ends.

# Revision Summary

*Ming-orama. The Victorians were awful. Worthy, moral, nice buildings but...oh dear. Going swimming wearing a small tent, throwing poor people in workhouses, singing patriotic songs all the blimmin' time and believing all sorts of bizarre medical theories about the size of women's brains. Not on your nelly. But for key stage three history purposes you have to learn about these weirdos — and what better way than answering this remarkably short and inviting list of questions...*

1) What was the Industrial Revolution?
2) What happened to the size of the British population between 1800 and 1850?
3) Which three of the following changed dramatically because of the Industrial Revolution?
   i) transport        ii) bed and breakfasts      iii) farming
   iv) post-it notes      v) industry           vi) tile and slate companies
4) Write a short paragraph to explain why the changes of the Industrial Revolution didn't affect everywhere in Britain at once.
5) Why did some protestors smash factory machines?
6) How did the authorities punish people who protested against the changes of the Industrial Revolution?
7) Write a short paragraph to explain why the middle class grew during the 1800s.
8) Describe three types of leisure activities enjoyed by the Victorian middle classes.
9) What is 'civic pride'?
10) What was the main reason for the expansion of the British Empire during the 1600s and 1700s?
11) What was Benjamin Disraeli's attitude to the British Empire?
12) How did British people celebrate the Empire?
13) How did the British East India Company gain land in India?
14) Describe two different views of what happened in the 'Black Hole of Calcutta'.
15) Explain how explorers and adventurers helped to expand the British Empire.
16) When did the 'Scramble for Africa' take place?
17) Give one positive and one negative effect of missionary activity.
18) Name three examples of wars where Britain gained or lost colonies.
19) List the Chartist's Six Points.
20) Did the Chartist movement campaign for women's voting rights?
21) Who was now allowed to vote under the 1867 Reform Act?
22) Write down four ways women's status improved during the 1850-1900 period.
23) What methods did Emmeline Pankhurst use to campaign for women's rights?
   a) organising campaign groups, stone throwing, hunger strikes
   b) using her influence as a liberal MP, letter-writing, speeches in Hyde Park
   c) marching the corridors of Whitehall, dressed as a monkey
24) Explain the difference between the suffragists' campaigning methods and the suffragettes' campaigning methods?
25) How did the First World War help get women the vote?
26) Is the following sentence true or false? "The Republicans in Ireland support British rule in Ireland."
27) Explain how the following events resulted in Irish resentment of the British —
   a) Oliver Cromwell's military involvement in Ireland in the 1600s
   b) The Great Famine of 1845-46
28) When was Ireland partitioned?
29) Describe what happened on 'Bloody Sunday' in Ireland in 1972.
30) What is 'ming-orama'?
   a) an entire panorama of ming
   b) armour built to withstand mingers
   c) a whole bunch of stinky cheese

# Islam & the Abbasid Empire

In the 500s, the people who lived in Arabia belonged to hundreds of different religions. Islam brought them together. Eventually most of the Middle East was part of one Muslim empire.

## Muhammad Founded Islam

1) Muhammad was born at Mecca, in Arabia, in 570. In 610 Muhammad started seeing visions — he saw an angel bringing messages from God (Allah).
2) Muhammad believed he should pass these messages on and began preaching to people in Mecca.
3) The things Muhammad said built up into a new religion — Islam. By the time he died in 632, it was followed by most people in Arabia.

- The angel's messages from Allah were written in a holy book called the Quran.
- Muhammad's sayings were written in a group of books called the Hadith.
- Muslims have five "pillars of faith".

SHAHADAH — belief in Allah and the Prophets
SALAT — praying five times a day
ZAKAT — paying a religious tax to help the poor
SAWM — fasting in the month called Ramadan
HAJJ — making a pilgrimage to Mecca

## The Caliph Ruled the Islamic Countries

1) After Muhammad died, Islam still needed a leader. Muslims chose Muhammad's father-in-law Abu Bakr. His title was Caliph — he was thought of as Muhammad's deputy.
2) The second Caliph was called Umar. He reigned from 634-644.
3) He fought wars in Palestine, Syria, and Egypt, and spread Islam into these countries.

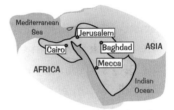

Islam in 644. Baghdad was just a little village at this time.

## Baghdad was the Capital of the Abbasid Empire

The Caliphs built up an Empire — it's sometimes called the Abbasid Empire. In 762 Caliph al-Munsur decided to build a new capital for his empire at Baghdad.

1) Baghdad was on a fertile plain with lots of rivers — food and water were no problem.
2) There were wide streets, which were lit up at night.
3) Aqueducts brought water into the town for homes and gardens.
4) Rubbish was cleared out of the city.
5) Philosophy, science and medicine were all studied and discussed. The House of Wisdom — a kind of library — was built in 832.
6) Images of people and animals aren't allowed in Islam — but artists made beautiful geometrical paintings and carvings, and used writing to make decorative patterns.

Merchants live outside city walls. Bazaars are here too.

Most people live here

Caliph's palace

City walls

Parks and gardens. Army barracks round the edge.

Baghdad was rich and successful for hundreds of years. Then in 1252, Mongols led by Hulagu, a grandson of Genghis Khan, captured and burned the city. This was the end of the Abbasid Empire.

## Baghdad, Baghmum and all the baby Baghs...

From one bloke preaching in Mecca to a religion spread all over the Middle East, plus an empire with a corking great capital built from scratch — all within a hundred and fifty odd years. That's pretty impressive. It must have taken quite an effort. Makes me feel tired just thinking about it.

# Christians v. Muslims — The Crusades

Muslims and Christians kept fighting over Jerusalem. It was a holy city for both sides as well as for Jews. It doesn't seem all that holy to have <u>bloodthirsty wars</u> all the time, mind.

## The <u>Crusaders</u> <u>wanted</u> <u>Control</u> of <u>Jerusalem</u>

Jerusalem had been part of the Abbasid Empire since 637. Then in <u>1055</u> Jerusalem was <u>captured</u> by the <u>Seljuk Turks</u>. They made it difficult and <u>dangerous</u> for <u>Christian pilgrims</u> to visit the city.

1099 — First Crusade
1148 — Second Crusade
1187 — Battle of Hattin
1189-92 — Third Crusade
1202 — Fourth Crusade

1) The Christian ruler of the <u>Byzantine Empire</u> was afraid the Turks would attack his lands next. He asked <u>Pope Urban II</u> for help. In 1095 the Pope called for a <u>Crusade</u>.

2) <u>Thousands</u> of people joined the Crusade — mostly ordinary people and the poorer nobles. The army reached Jerusalem in <u>June 1099</u>. After an eight-day siege they took the city.

3) The Crusaders set up a new kingdom — the <u>Latin Kingdom of Jerusalem</u>. Many crusaders got land and <u>stayed on</u> in the Middle East.

There was a <u>Second Crusade</u> in <u>1148</u>, but it didn't achieve much.

*Jerusalem*

## <u>Saladin</u>* Recaptured Jerusalem

*\* this is Saladin Salah ad-Din Yusuf in Arabic*

1) Saladin lived 1138-1193. He was a <u>tough soldier</u> in charge of the <u>Syrian and Egyptian armies</u>. He was also known as a <u>fair</u>, <u>generous man</u> who built colleges, mosques and hospitals in Cairo.

2) In 1187 Saladin led an army to <u>Hattin</u>, in Galilee, where the King of Jerusalem's army was camped. Saladin's forces destroyed the entire Christian army in one day and went on to <u>take Jerusalem</u>.

3) A Third Crusade was sent to push Saladin out in 1189. The Christian army, led by Richard I of England, <u>didn't</u> win back Jerusalem, but they did recapture some ports along the coast, e.g. Acre.

## The <u>Fourth Crusade</u> Never Made it to Jerusalem

1) In 1198 Pope Innocent III called for <u>another crusade</u>. 11,000 Crusaders met in <u>Venice</u> in 1202.

2) The Crusaders attacked a <u>Christian</u> port called Zara and then <u>Constantinople</u> — the Christian capital of the Byzantine Empire.

3) The Crusaders spent <u>3 days</u> looting and destroying Constantinople.

4) The fourth crusade petered out <u>without reaching Jerusalem</u>.

5) Eventually the Latin Kingdom fell apart — <u>Acre</u> was lost in <u>1291</u>.

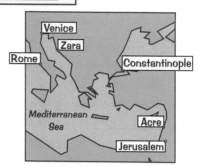

## The <u>Ottoman Empire</u> Grew in the Eastern Mediterranean

1) A new Islamic empire, called the <u>Ottoman Empire</u>, was growing in eastern Turkey.

2) In <u>1453</u> the Ottoman ruler <u>Sultan Mehmed</u> captured Constantinople and made it his capital.

3) The Ottoman's greatest ruler was <u>Suleyman the Magnificent</u> (1520-1566). He was a wise lawgiver and encouraged <u>religious tolerance</u> — Christians were given important jobs in government.

## <u>Pope Urban II — comin' atcha...</u>

There's something very fishy about that last Crusade. I mean, they didn't get anywhere near Jerusalem AND they spent all their time sacking Christian cities. But Venice got control of two major trading ports, so they could do lots of trade and make themselves even richer. Hmmm...

# The Mughal Empire

The first Mughal was Babur. He built up an empire in India which ended up being ruled by his family for over 150 years. That's even longer than Tony Blair's been at 10 Downing Street.

## Babur was the First Mughal Emperor

Babur grew up in Ferghana (now in Tajikistan). Like most nobles in the region he was a Muslim, descended from Genghis Khan — leader of the Mongols and ruler of the world's biggest empire ever.

1) As a young man he captured Samarkand (Uzbekistan) and Kabul (Afghanistan) before going on to India.

2) In India he took Delhi and Agra and became Sultan. He ruled in India from 1526 until 1530.

3) Babur was a highly skilled military leader with an army of around 10,000 men. He used muskets and artillery — pretty technologically advanced for the time.

4) After Babur's death, his son Humayun ruled the Kingdom. Humayun wasn't such a great leader and was eventually driven out of India by Sher Shah.

## Akbar's Government was Tolerant and Well-Organised

1) Akbar was Babur's grandson. He had to invade India all over again. He won so much territory that his kingdom was bigger than Babur's.

2) Akbar was crowned on Feb 15th 1556.

3) His government was tolerant — local Hindu rulers got jobs alongside Akbar's friends and family.

4) He encouraged a new religion called the 'Divine Faith' which included bits of Islam and Hinduism.

5) Akbar developed trade links and set up a system of weights and measures (good for trade because it means people can't be cheated so they're more willing to buy stuff).

6) He set up a fair but efficient tax system.

7) Even though Akbar probably couldn't read himself, he encouraged scholars and writers.

1483 — Babur born
1526 — Babur crowned
1530 — Humayun crowned
1556 — Akbar crowned
1605 — Jahangir crowned
1627 — Shah Jahan crowned
1658 — Aurangzeb crowned

Babur means "The Tiger"
Akbar means "The Great"

See p46 for Aurangzeb

## The Mughals Loved Art and Architecture

Mughal architecture was a mixture of Indian and Persian styles.

*Taj Mahal*

1) Buildings had arched doorways, arched windows and massive domes.

2) Akbar built a whole new capital outside Delhi called Fatehpur Sikri.

3) Shah Jahan built the Taj Mahal at Agra as a tomb for his wife Mumtaz.

The Mughals were mad about gardens. They were laid out in patterns and always had lots of fountains and running water. Babur loved his garden in Kabul so much that he was taken all the way back there to be buried.

Muslims weren't supposed to make art of people or animals — but under the Mughals Indian painters developed a beautiful detailed style of miniatures. They painted portraits and scientific studies of animals.

## Babur — isn't he a small French elephant?...

Shah Jahan wanted to put a black tomb for himself opposite the white one for Mumtaz, but he ran out of time. When I went to the Taj Mahal there were hundreds of newly-weds there having their photos taken — because it's all so romantic I suppose. Aaahhhh.../Retch, retch.*

*(Delete as applicable)*

# Aurangzeb — The Last Mughal

The Mughals were the tiger's whiskers for 150 years — but it couldn't last forever.
After Aurangzeb died, things began to <u>fall apart</u>.

## Aurangzeb was the Last Mughal Emperor

1) In 1658 Aurangzeb <u>fought</u> and defeated his brothers, <u>imprisoned</u> his father, Shah Jahan, and <u>took the throne</u>.

2) Aurangzeb was a <u>committed Muslim</u>. He didn't tolerate <u>other religions</u> — he persecuted Hindus and had a Sikh guru executed.

1658 — Aurangzeb rebels and becomes Emperor.
early 1660s — Shivaji rebels against Aurangzeb.
1664 — Shivaji takes Surat and builds kingdom.
1680 — Shivaji dies.
1707 — Aurangzeb dies.

## Aurangzeb Put All his Energy into Fighting Rebels

Aurangzeb had major problems because of a Hindu lord called <u>Shivaji</u>. Shivaji's father was an important Hindu noble in the region of <u>Bijapur</u>, which was ruled by the Moghuls. When he was 16, Shivaji took a pledge to set up an <u>independent Hindu state</u>.

1) In the early 1660s Shivaji started a <u>rebellion</u> against Afzal Khan — Aurangzeb's general in charge of Bijapur.

2) Afzal Khan put down the rebellion and arranged to <u>meet</u> Shivaji to discuss terms. They weren't meant to be armed, but Shivaji came to the meeting wearing <u>steel tiger claws</u> on his fingers, and killed Afzal Khan by slashing open his stomach.

3) In 1664 Shivaji captured the city of <u>Surat</u>. He was now <u>ruler</u> of his region.

4) Shivaji agreed to acknowledge Aurangzeb as <u>overall</u> ruler — but it didn't take long before he was <u>rebelling</u> again.

5) Shivaji created a unified <u>Hindu state</u> which lasted till he died in 1680. He's still thought of as a <u>hero</u> by many Hindus in India today.

Aurangzeb spent the last 20 years of his life marching round India <u>dealing with rebels</u>. When he died in 1707 there was nobody <u>strong enough</u> to hold the Empire together.

## India Became Part of the British Empire

1) The British <u>East India Company</u> started trading in India in the 1600s.
2) The Company built <u>forts</u> and kept <u>private armies</u> because of rivalry with French traders.
3) After Aurangzeb died in 1707, the British used these armies to <u>spread</u> their territories from the coastal cities like Calcutta, Bombay and Madras into the old Mughal lands.
4) The East India Company ran India like a <u>mini-government</u> until, in 1857, Indian troops <u>rebelled</u> at the increasing power of the British.
5) The rebellion was put down, but the British Government decided the East India Company wasn't up to running the country. India was made an official part of the <u>British Empire</u>.

## Rebels are chocolate coated — oh hang on that's revels...

Aurangzeb's empire was massive by the time he died — it almost reached to the very south of India. But he had a blooming hard job keeping it all going. Make sure you take in all the stuff about Shivaji — he kind of proves that the Mughals weren't invincible. Unlike Spiderman.

# Africa & the Slave Trade

Millions and millions of people were taken from West Africa between the 1400s and 1700s, and sold as slaves — mainly in the West Indies and North and South America.

## Slavery's Been Around Since the Beginning of History

1) In Ancient Greece slaves worked in mines, on farms and as house servants.
2) The Roman Empire would have ground to a halt without slavery — at times there were more slaves in Rome than there were Romans.
3) In the 600s the Abbasid Empire (see p.43) enslaved black Africans.

## There Was Some Slavery in Africa Before Europeans Came

The Songhay Empire was the most important in West Africa in the 1400s.

Europeans started coming to West Africa in about 1415. At that time most Africans lived by either herding animals, growing crops or trading.

1) Many West African tribes kept slaves. Most were prisoners of war.
2) Some were kept in chains and worked hard.
3) Others lived as part of the family they worked for, and could earn their freedom over time, or be bought back by their own families.
4) Before Europeans arrived, Muslim traders sold about 5,000 people a year into slavery in Europe and the Middle East.

## European Slavery Was on a Massive Scale

The Portuguese were the first Europeans to reach West Africa in about 1415. They were looking for a trade route to India — they wanted to buy spices without going through expensive Arab middlemen.

1) The Portuguese started trading for slaves to work on their plantations in Madeira and the Canary Islands.
2) After Columbus found the West Indies in 1492, the Spanish set up plantations there.
3) The Portuguese started selling slaves to the Spanish. They were made to work in the plantations.
4) By the 1600s, the British, Dutch and French had set up trade posts in Africa to sell slaves to the Spanish.
5) By the 1700s the British dominated the transatlantic slave trade and had plantations of their own in the West Indies and America.
6) At least 11 million people died on the way across the Atlantic because of atrocious conditions and treatment. Many millions more became slaves.

The plantations grew crops like cotton, tobacco and sugar, which the plantation owners could sell for big profits back in Europe.

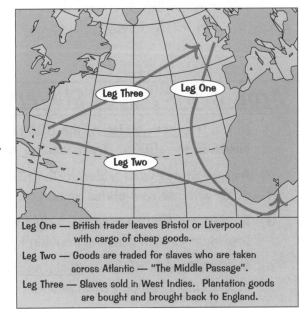

Leg One — British trader leaves Bristol or Liverpool with cargo of cheap goods.
Leg Two — Goods are traded for slaves who are taken across Atlantic — "The Middle Passage".
Leg Three — Slaves sold in West Indies. Plantation goods are bought and brought back to England.

The British trade across the Atlantic is known as 'the Triangular Trade'.

## What doesn't kill us makes us stronger — that's the theory...

Here's another cheery thought — slavery still hasn't died out completely. There are still bits of the Middle East and Africa where people buy and sell slaves — and they're mainly children. On the positive side, oh no, there isn't a positive side. I'm sorry, my mistake.

# The End of Slavery

Slavery eventually got banned in Britain and the USA, but it was a tough fight. Plantation owners were making a lot of money from slavery and wanted to <u>carry on</u> making a lot of money.

## Slaves Lived and Died in Terrible Conditions

1) People were snatched from their villages by African slavers and <u>sold</u> to white European traders as slaves.

2) The slaves were crammed onto <u>ships</u> where they were <u>chained</u> in rows, and had to lie in each other's vomit and waste for weeks on end as the ships crossed the Atlantic.

3) In the West Indies and North America, slaves were sold to <u>plantation owners</u> and set to work in the cotton, tobacco or sugarcane fields.

4) The work and conditions were incredibly <u>harsh</u> and slaves rarely lived beyond their <u>20s</u>.

*Sugarcane has sharp jagged leaves that can easily cut skin.*

## People Started to Fight Against Slavery

1) Some slaves protested by making things difficult for their owners — <u>breaking tools</u> and <u>destroying crops</u> were good ways to disrupt business.

2) Slaves on the plantations sometimes <u>ran away</u>. It was dangerous because they could be severely punished or even killed if they were caught.

3) In the USA an organisation called <u>The Underground Railroad</u> smuggled escaped slaves to the <u>Northern states</u>, where there was no slavery.

In Britain, men like <u>William Wilberforce</u> and <u>Granville Sharp</u> fought against slavery in the courts and Parliament.

In the British Empire the <u>slave trade</u> was banned in 1807. <u>Keeping slaves</u> was banned in 1833.

*Olaudah Equiano was a slave, captured at the age of 11. He escaped and published his life story. This helped people like William Wilberforce gain support for his campaign.*

## Arguments About Slavery in the USA Started a Civil War

1) In the <u>Southern states</u> of the USA plantation owners still had slaves in the <u>1850s</u>. There was <u>no slavery</u> in the <u>Northern states</u>.

2) As <u>new states</u> were added to the USA there were big debates as to whether new states should be <u>slave</u> states or <u>free</u> states.

3) In 1861 the Southern states, called the <u>Confederacy</u>, left the Union. President Lincoln said they couldn't and <u>civil war</u> broke out.

4) In 1863 Lincoln declared <u>all slaves free</u> in the Emancipation Proclamation.

■ The Northern (Union) States — Against slavery
■ Border States — For slavery, but loyal to the North
□ The Southern (Confederate) States — For slavery

5) The <u>North</u> won the Civil war in 1865. The Southern states had to stay in the USA, and the Constitution was changed — the <u>13th Amendment</u> banned slavery.

## "I seem to have shot you", "Oh dear" — what a civil war...

It all sounds quite quick if you read about it on an A4 bit of paper — but it wasn't quick at all. From the first slaves taken by the Portuguese in the 1400s to slavery getting banned in the USA was over four hundred years. That's <u>four hundred years</u> of people living and dying as slaves.

# The Civil Rights Movement

Life didn't suddenly become <u>easy</u> for black people in the USA when slavery ended.
Most black people still had <u>less rights</u> and <u>harder lives</u> than most white people.

## In the South Black People's Lives Didn't Improve Much

After the Civil War, the Northern government rushed in <u>food and medicine</u> to
help the southern whites and blacks, and radicals in the US government tried
to take power from the white southerners in order to <u>help</u> black people, <u>BUT</u>...

Ku Klux Klan

1) White Southern politicians introduced laws called the <u>Black Codes</u>
which made it hard for black people to leave the plantations.
2) The <u>Ku Klux Klan</u> was formed. It was a secret organisation
meant to keep black people down using <u>violence and terror</u>.
3) When US troops left the South in 1877 the <u>Jim Crow laws</u> were passed.
These laws meant that black people and white people were kept apart —
this is called <u>segregation</u>.

## The Civil Rights Movement Formed to Fight Segregation

<u>Segregation</u> meant black people had very poor civil rights,
though on paper they were meant to have <u>equal rights</u>.

> <u>Civil rights</u> = good, <u>equal</u> treatment for all
> citizens whatever their colour,
> race, religion or other beliefs

1) Segregation was meant to separate people but treat them
<u>equally</u>. In reality, black people had much <u>poorer living conditions</u> and schools than white people.
2) In the <u>First World War</u>, black people fought for their country and contributed to the war effort at
home, but were <u>not allowed</u> to join white units, join the marines, or become naval officers.
3) In the <u>Second World War</u>, black people fought for America again, but when they came home to
the Southern states they still had to live with segregation. They were even <u>prevented from voting</u>.
4) The National Association for the Advancement of Coloured People (<u>NAACP</u>) had formed in 1909
and began campaigning for <u>Civil Rights</u>.
5) The breakthrough came in <u>1954</u> when a law was passed to allow
<u>black and white children</u> to attend the <u>same schools</u>. However,
many Southern States <u>ignored</u> this and other Civil Rights laws.

## The Civil Rights Bill Ended Segregation

The Civil Rights movement was led by people like <u>Martin Luther King</u> and <u>Malcolm X</u>.

> *Martin Luther King
> used non-violent
> tactics similar to
> those used by
> Mahatma Gandhi to
> bring about change.
> He was assassinated
> in Memphis,
> Tennessee in 1968.*

> *Malcolm X led the
> Black Power
> movement to use
> stronger action to
> improve conditions for
> blacks after the Civil
> Rights movement.
> He was assassinated
> in 1965.*

1) In <u>1955</u> a black woman called <u>Rosa Parks</u> refused to
stand up on a bus just so that a white man could sit
down. She was arrested. Black people <u>boycotted
the buses</u> and ended laws on bus segregation.
2) The Civil Rights movement used tactics such as
<u>sit-ins</u>, <u>freedom rides</u>, <u>boycotts</u> and <u>marches</u> to bring
about an end to segregation in a <u>non-violent</u> way.
3) In <u>1964</u> the <u>Civil Rights Bill</u> was passed which ended
segregation in the USA.

## Good old civil rights Bill — he sure is a busy guy...

The Civil Rights Bill was a huge step. But it didn't solve all the race problems in America — it was
only the beginning of a huge fight. It's pretty scary that a nation like America could be capable of
such intense racism, while at the same time claiming to give equal rights to all its citizens.

# Adolf Hitler — Totalitarian Ruler

Totalitarian rulers have so much power that they can make people do whatever they want.
Hitler's an example of a totalitarian ruler — he used all that power to do some terrible things.

## Hitler Created a Totalitarian State

*A totalitarian state is where the government has complete control of a country. The people have no say in how it's run. The government controls the press and there's no freedom of speech. Human rights are usually lost by many citizens.*

When Adolf Hitler and the Nazis came to power in 1933, they created a totalitarian state. Human rights were not important to Hitler.

1) Political prisoners were held in concentration camps.
2) Hitler tried to "purify" German blood by locking up gypsies, homosexuals, alcoholics and the mentally and physically handicapped in concentration camps.
3) Many of these people were systematically killed.
4) However it was the Jews who Hitler was particularly keen to eliminate.

## Hitler Hated the Jews

Jews were seen by Hitler as a very distinct social group.
He held them responsible for Germany's problems.

1) During his rise to power, Hitler blamed the Jews for Germany's economic problems and defeat in World War I.
2) He used his storm troopers, the SA, to stir up hatred towards the Jews.
3) Hitler used propaganda in newspapers and newsreels to increase the hatred towards Jews.

Adolf Hitler

*Propaganda = information (sometimes invented) presented in a way that is meant to influence and manipulate people's way of thinking*

## The Jews Were Gradually Persecuted

When he came to power Hitler began to systematically persecute the Jews.

1) After he came to power, attacks on Jews increased. Jews were banned from professional jobs in such things as medicine and law.
2) In 1935, The Nuremberg Laws banned Jews from marrying non-Jews. The Reich Citizenship Laws removed their right to vote and their protection by the law.
3) By 1938, the Jews were banned from public places.
4) On the Night of Broken Glass, Kristallnacht, Jewish shops and synagogues were smashed. Over 20,000 Jewish men were sent to concentration camps.

*Concentration camps were a British invention, used during the Boer War at the beginning of the 20th Century. They were a way of locking up enemies of the state, usually in poor conditions resulting in a high death rate.*

**Hitler's Persecution of the Jews**

1933 — Mass persecution began with the boycott of Jewish shops and businesses.

1935 — Reich Citizenship Laws.

1935 — Nuremberg Laws.

1938 — Kristallnacht, night of broken glass.

1938 — Jews banned from public places.

1939 — Jews captured in Poland were shut up into ghettos such as Warsaw in appalling conditions.

## Totalitarianism means there's no freedom of speech...

That means that people who speak out against the government get arrested, or worse. So if you're being persecuted, there's really not much at all you can do about it.

# Ghettos and Anne Frank

Ghetto is a word which means an area of a city inhabited by members of a particular racial group, usually in poor living conditions. In 1940 the Nazis gave it a more sinister meaning.

## The Jews Had to Live in Ghettos

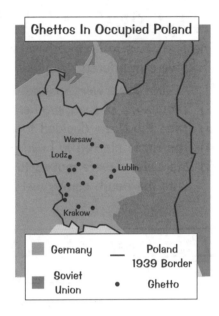

Ghettos In Occupied Poland

1) Originally, the Nazis were going to create a reservation for Jews near Lublin in Poland.

2) However, they quickly changed their minds and started to wall off areas of cities to house the Jews.

3) These areas were called ghettos. The biggest was in Warsaw.

4) Conditions in these overcrowded slums were terrible, with hundreds of thousands dying.

Warsaw
Lodz
Lublin
Krakow

Germany — Poland 1939 Border
Soviet Union • Ghetto

> ### Conditions in the Ghetto
> Whole families were crowded into each room. The Jews were given a handful of bread each day. If they tried to leave the Ghetto they were murdered. The German people were shown newsreels of Jews being resettled in good conditions. Diseases like dysentery and typhus killed those people already weakened by hunger.

## The Germans Took Holland in May 1940

1) The Germans took control of Amsterdam and the rest of Holland in May 1940.
2) The Jews living in Holland were soon made to live under similar rules to the German Jews.
3) Many Jews were deported to Germany to work in forced labour camps. Many disappeared.

## The Franks Were a Jewish Family Who Hid From The Nazis

The Frank family were Jewish. They originally lived in Germany but then moved to Amsterdam to get away from the Nazis. Then the Nazis invaded the Netherlands. In July 1942, Otto Frank took his family into hiding in a building attached to his office. His daughter Anne kept a diary of the events.

1) Some brave friends brought them food and kept the hiding place secret.

2) The Franks stayed in the secret annexe, with another family and friend, until 1944, when the allied liberating forces were close by.

3) But the annexe was raided by the SS on 4th August 1944 and the inhabitants were all sent to concentration camps.

4) Anne and her sister Margot died within a few days of each other in Bergen-Belsen, about a month before the camp was liberated by the allies. Otto Frank was the only survivor.

5) Anne's diary was found by the family's friends, who gave it to Otto when he returned. Otto Frank published the diary in 1947.

Anne Frank's diary was published in 1947. It was translated into English in 1951 and has sold millions of copies, helping publicise the horror of the Holocaust.

## Anne Frank was 13 years old when she went into hiding...

The people in the secret annexe hid there for over two years — just imagine...
You couldn't go outside at all. And all the time outside your window people would be running, hiding, killing, dying... Makes me feel pretty lucky to be alive today, you know.

# The Final Solution

When Adolf Hitler met with the senior members of the Nazi party in 1941, they planned the 'Final Solution' to the Jewish Problem — the complete annihilation of a race of people. This is called genocide.

## The Einsatzgruppen Shot Many Jews

The first Jews to be murdered were the Polish and Russian Jews.
They were murdered by special units of SS called Einsatzgruppen.

1) At first Jews were taken out and made to dig their own graves before being shot.
2) Thousands of men, women and children were shot in this way.
3) Then the Nazis decided they wanted to speed up this process.
4) The Nazis started to build death camps at places such as Treblinka and Auschwitz-Birkenau.
5) Many Jews were moved to the ghettos at places such as Lodz and Warsaw where they were kept until the death camps were ready.

## The Final Solution Began in March 1942

In March 1942, the Final Solution began in earnest at Auschwitz-Birkenau.

1) Auschwitz-Birkenau was a dual purpose camp — Auschwitz was a labour camp, but Birkenau was a death camp.
2) On their arrival by train, the Jews were divided into two groups — those fit to work (although they were virtually worked to death), and those unfit to work (like children or the elderly) who would be gassed straight away.
3) Those chosen to die were calmly told to undress. They were shaved and told they were going to have a shower. Once in the shower, they were killed with Zyklon B, a poisonous gas.
4) The bodies were then cremated after gold teeth had been pulled out and jewellery removed.

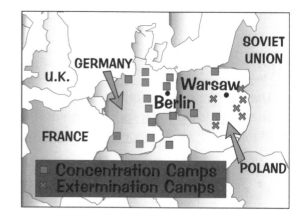

## The Final Solution Murdered Over Six Million People

In 1945, Allied soldiers began to liberate the camps and could not believe the horror they found.

1) The Allied solders were overwhelmed by the scenes of death and near death they witnessed.
2) Over six million had been murdered mechanically by the Nazi regime — Jews, gypsies, political prisoners, homosexuals, handicapped people, and prisoners of war were all victims of the Nazis.
3) Many of the Germans who had run the death camps were brought to justice at the Nuremberg Trials after the war.
4) Hitler shot himself in a bunker in Berlin at the end of the war in 1945.

> People have come up with their own different responses to the Holocaust. Some people try to pretend it didn't happen.
> Some people have concluded that there is no God, or that if there is one, he doesn't care about us.
> Other people use it as a lesson, to promote kindness and try to make sure that it never ever happens again.

## Over 6 million people died...

More than 6 million people died. More than 6 million. It's worth taking the time to think about it.

# Twentieth Century Wars Made by Machines

In the twentieth century inventions like aeroplanes and nuclear bombs made it easier to kill more people more quickly. War changed from mainly affecting armies to involving armies <u>and</u> civilians.

## Technology _changed_ Tactics _in WW1_

The <u>generals</u> who fought the <u>First World War</u> expected to do so using the <u>tactics</u> of the <u>last one</u> — cavalry charges, infantry charges and sword fights. They were wrong — technology had moved on.

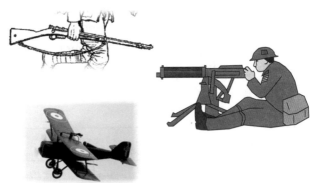

1) <u>Breach-loading rifles</u> meant soldiers could <u>reload rapidly</u> whilst <u>lying down</u>. Machine guns made it possible to fire <u>hundreds</u> of bullets a minute.

2) <u>Breach-loading artillery</u> and <u>machine-guns</u> meant that moving about in the open was now <u>suicidal</u>.

3) All this meant that <u>defence</u> was now much <u>more important</u> than <u>attack</u>. Soldiers spent more time digging <u>trenches</u> and defending them, and less time charging across battlefields.

## Technology _advanced_ further

With soldiers relatively secure in trenches, <u>new ways</u> of attacking them were needed.

### Twentieth Century Wars
1914 to 1918 — World War I
1918 to 1921 — Russian Civil War
1936 — Spanish Civil War
1939 to 1945 — World War II
1950 to 1953 — Korean War
1963 to 1973 — Vietnam War
1991 — Gulf War

1) <u>Poison gas</u> and <u>tanks</u> were developed to overcome strong defences. This led to another <u>change in tactics</u> which made <u>attacking</u> worthwhile again.

2) During the <u>Second World War</u> Hitler used a combination of tanks, aircraft and motorised infantry to smash through defences. This was called <u>Blitzkrieg</u> — 'lightning war'.

3) By the <u>end</u> of the Second World War, <u>nuclear weapons</u> had changed warfare for ever — <u>whole cities</u> could now be <u>destroyed</u> by a single bomb.

## Civilians _Have Become_ More and More Involved _in Wars_

1) During the First World War, <u>cities</u> were <u>bombed</u> from the air by aeroplanes and airships. The aim was to <u>destroy factories</u> and make it harder for the enemy to make the stuff they needed to win the war. Factories are usually round towns so lots of <u>civilians</u> got killed. Bombing cities like this is sometimes called "<u>Total War</u>".

2) During the <u>Second World War</u>, whole <u>cities</u> such as Coventry and Dresden were bombed into rubble. Civilians also suffered from <u>food rationing</u> and <u>starvation</u>. Armies deliberately attacked civilians because they realised it would weaken the <u>morale</u> of their enemies.

3) After the war, civilians began to take more of a critical role in deciding if wars should happen at all. There were <u>mass protests</u> against the Vietnam War (1961-75) and smaller ones against the Gulf war (1991) and Kosovo (1999).

## Technology has advanced — but do we have lightsabers?...

Modern warfare is scary stuff. In fact all warfare is scary stuff. Whoever has the most soldiers and weapons wins. But do they deserve to? That's a question to keep you awake at night...

# The Nuclear Age

It was not until the twentieth century that mankind achieved the capability to destroy the planet.

## Nuclear Weapons — The Most Powerful Weapons... Ever

On 16th July 1945, US scientists successfully tested a nuclear bomb in the New Mexico desert.

1) In WW2, the Americans suffered enormous casualties attacking the Japanese island of Okinawa. They realised that attacking Japan itself would cost them hundreds of thousands of Americans.

2) President Truman decided that it would be better to end the war quickly by using nuclear weapons.

3) On 6th August 1945 a nuclear bomb was dropped on Hiroshima, Japan. On 9th August a second bomb was dropped on Nagasaki.

4) 120,000 people were killed by the two bombs, with half a million dying later from radiation poisoning.

## The Iron Curtain Divided Democratic West & Communist East

After the Second World War ended, the leaders of the three big allied powers met at Potsdam to decide on the future of Europe, but all was not well.

1) The leader of the Soviet Union, Joseph Stalin, did not want to move his troops out of the countries of Eastern Europe that he controlled.

2) By 1946, many countries such as Poland, Hungary, Romania and Albania had communist governments, backed by Stalin.

3) In 1946, Winston Churchill made a speech in which he said that from Stettin in the Baltic to Trieste in the Adriatic, an Iron Curtain had descended across the continent.

4) This Iron Curtain divided Europe between the Democratic West and Communist East for almost 50 years.

## The Cold War — the US and USSR Never Fought Directly

The Cold War never led to direct conflict between the East and West — the two sides were too scared of nuclear war. But the conflict was fought all round the world as the two sides supported rival governments in Africa and Asia, e.g. in Vietnam.

1) The western powers formed an alliance, NATO, the North Atlantic Treaty Organisation. The communists formed the Warsaw Pact.

2) An arms race followed, with the two sides trying to produce more and better nuclear weapons.

3) The Americans were terrified of the spread of communism outside Europe and tried to stop it everywhere it appeared.

4) Both sides mistrusted each other and used spies to steal each other's secrets.

5) Eventually, communism came to an end because it failed to keep pace economically with the free economies of the West.

| | |
|---|---|
| — | Iron Curtain |
| | Warsaw Pact 1955 |
| | Communist but neutral |
| | NATO |
| 1950 | Date of joining NATO |

ICELAND 1949
CANADA 1949
USA 1949
NORWAY 1949  SWEDEN  FINLAND
DENMARK 1949
EIRE  BRITAIN 1949  NETHERLANDS 1949
BELGIUM 1949  EAST GERMANY  POLAND
WEST GERMANY 1955  CZECHOSLOVAKIA  USSR
FRANCE 1949  SWITZ.  AUSTRIA  HUNGARY
PORTUGAL 1949  SPAIN 1982  ITALY 1949  YUGOSLAVIA  ROMANIA
BULGARIA
GREECE 1952  TURKEY 1952
ALBANIA Expelled in 1968

## The cold war — so much as sneeze and I'll blow you away...

It's pretty hard to think about what that level of paranoia must have felt like. The world was on the brink of nuclear war. If it hadn't been for ordinary people protesting, maybe we wouldn't be here now.

# Scientific Advances

The history of science goes back to prehistoric people — we know they had some science knowledge, as they were able to build monuments such as Stonehenge in alignment with the sun.

## Egyptians and Greeks Knew About Astronomy

It's only when people from the past write things down that we can get a really good idea about what they knew and thought.

1) The Egyptians believed in many gods. They thought the gods controlled everything they didn't understand.
2) The Egyptians had a good knowledge of astronomy (study of the stars and the universe).
3) The Greeks also had a complex mythology to explain how their set of gods controlled their world.
4) Later Greek philosophers (such as Archimedes) explained the world in terms of mathematics and balance.
5) Aristotle produced a model of the solar system with the earth as the centre.

Ancient Egypt

Ancient Greece

## The Catholic Church Prevented Scientific Advancement

Greek theories about science and medicine lasted for 1500 years, until the Renaissance — a 'rebirth' of science and culture in the 15th and 16th centuries.

A long time ago, in a galaxy far, far away...

1) The Roman Catholic church supported the idea that the Earth was the centre of the universe. To disagree with the church was a crime called heresy, so very few people did.
2) In 1514, Copernicus (scared of the church) privately published his ideas that actually the Sun was the centre of the universe.
3) In the 17th century, Galileo used a telescope to study the planets. His findings agreed with those of Copernicus.
4) When Galileo published his ideas, he got locked up for heresy straight away.
5) Because of the Roman Catholic Church's opposition, astronomy was strongest in Protestant countries.

## Scientific Advances Were Made in Britain

In 1660 the Royal Society was set up in England to study the natural world. All the best scientists were asked to join.

1) Isaac Newton used his Theory of Gravity to explain why planets moved in their orbits. His scientific laws could be used to describe the movement of everything in the universe.
2) Robert Boyle worked out the basics of modern chemistry.
3) Robert Hooke, who worked with Boyle, discovered how things like springs stretch.

> Charles Darwin was a naturalist who developed the idea that living things evolved according to the laws of natural selection and survival of the fittest. He came up with it on a voyage of exploration around the world aboard HMS Beagle in 1831. He published his findings in a book called 'The Origin of Species' in 1859. His ideas were very controversial because they went against the teachings of the Bible. That's had a huge effect on modern thinking about science and religion.

 on...
Copper-knickers must have been one brainy bloke. He had guts n'all, risking prison and worse just so he could do a bit of science homework. So don't let any 500 year old Catholics see this book, OK?

# Science Helping People

Disease has been the human race's worst enemy for thousands of years. Throughout most of human history, nobody understood what caused diseases, let alone how to cure them.

## Infectious Diseases Killed Many People

The poor living conditions in medieval towns left their inhabitants open to attack by many different infectious diseases over the ages — lots of people died because no one knew how to cure them.

Germ Warfare

1) In the mid-1300s the Black Death came to Europe from the East and killed at least a third of the population.
2) Many different infectious diseases killed huge numbers of people over the next few centuries.
3) By the 1700s smallpox was the big killer.
4) At the start of the 1800s, a new killer cholera arrived in the industrial towns of Britain.

## Louis Pasteur Proved that Germs Cause Diseases

People used to believe in the idea of Spontaneous Generation. This said that disease was caused by poisonous gases called miasmas, and that germs were the result of disease.

1) Using the new microscopes, scientists knew that micro-organisms ( i.e. germs) existed, but didn't know that they caused disease.
2) In 1867, Louis Pasteur was able to prove that germs were the cause of disease. This was called Germ Theory.
3) In 1875, Robert Koch linked germ theory to a specific disease — Anthrax.

## Vaccines Were Developed to Prevent Diseases

The next stage was to be able to prevent a disease.
1) In 1796, an English doctor, Edward Jenner, discovered a vaccine against smallpox, but he didn't know how it worked.
2) In the 1880s Pasteur discovered vaccines against Chicken Cholera, Anthrax, and Rabies — he knew how they worked, because of his work with germ theory.
3) Vaccines for many other diseases such as Tuberculosis and Polio were discovered during the late 1800s and early 1900s.
4) The World Health Organisation, Red Cross and Red Crescent have used vaccination programmes to try and eliminate many diseases world wide.

## Science Has Also Been Used For Mass Destruction

1) Some Ancient Greeks believed that all matter was made up of tiny particles called atoms, which could not be broken down further.
2) In 1911, Ernest Rutherford produced a diagram of an atom.
3) In 1939, scientists in Germany and Italy succeeded in splitting the atom — this is called nuclear fission. It led to the creation of the first weapons of mass destruction.
4) In 1945 the first atomic bombs dropped on Japan, killing around 120,000 people.

## Did you get your flu jab last night? — just a shot in the dark...

Vaccines and atomic bombs... Science isn't good or bad, that bit's down to us.

# A Healthier World

People today are generally healthier than they were a hundred years ago.

## The Government Reformed the Public Health System

When the British government tried to recruit soldiers from the poorer classes to fight in the Boer wars in the late 1800s, it was horrified to discover the state of malnutrition and poor health that existed.

1) In 1903, Charles Booth produced a report which said that a third of people in London were living below the poverty line.
2) David Lloyd George's Liberal government decided to do something about it.
3) They introduced a series of reforms that laid the foundations of what was to become the Welfare State (Welfare state = the Government pays for pensions, health and welfare services).
4) In 1942 Sir William Beveridge produced a report identifying five giant wants (i.e. needs for public health).
5) As a result of this, the new Labour government introduced the Welfare state and the National Health Service in 1948 to tackle these wants.

*The NHS was received with great enthusiasm by the people. Some politicians such as Winston Churchill were worried that the country could not afford it. Doctors were not enthusiastic at first, because they thought they would lose their private income.*

## The 20th Century was a Healthier Century

Advances in technology and greater social awareness combined with better resources to make the 20th Century a much healthier time to live in.

1) Surgery improved greatly with new technology, good anaesthetics, antiseptics, improved surgical techniques and the introduction of blood transfusions.
2) Fleming, Florey and Chain's discovery of the world's first antibiotic, penicillin, in the mid 20th Century meant infection could be treated successfully for the first time.

*We really need a taller table...*

3) Vaccination programmes mean that people are no longer being killed by diseases of the past.
4) The Welfare State means that people have a better standard of living and a better diet.

## It's Not the Same in the Developing World

However, you have a much better chance of living longer in the developed world (e.g. Europe or America) than you have in the developing world (e.g. Africa or Indonesia).

1) In developing countries, people and governments have less money — they can't afford to spend as much as Western governments do on health care.
2) Organisations such as The World Health Organisation, The Red Cross, The Red Crescent and Medicins Sans Frontieres try to help developing countries.
3) A mass vaccination programme has eliminated smallpox and people are working to do the same with polio, malaria and tuberculosis.
4) However, sometimes medical help can be seen as interference by a country's government. It is also sometimes seen as an attempt by foreign governments to gain political influence.
5) Developing countries and global organisations like the World Health Organisation still have a massive task ahead of them.

## This book's History...
Well that's it. History in a nutshell. Last page of the section. Last section of the book. Woo-hoo.

# Revision Summary

*Well, that's the end of the book. Who would have thought you could cram so much information into such a skinny book? I guess we're going to get old and then die and then have history books written about us one day. I wonder what they'll write about us? The Twenty First Century — the century where everyone got fat eating burgers three times a day. Sheesh. What a depressing thought. Just do this final revision summary and get the history over and done with...*

1) Who was the founder of Islam?
2) What was a Caliph?  a) a fruity iced lolly   b) a leader or ruler   c) a mythical creature that was half man half goat
3) What was the capital of the Abbasid Empire?
4) What happened to Jerusalem in 1055?
5) Describe what happened in the first crusade in three sentences.
6) Who was Saladin, and what did he do in 1187?
7) Who was Babur?
8) Write a paragraph to explain what kind of government Akbar had.
9) Who built the Taj Mahal?
10) What kind of a ruler was Aurangzeb?   a) tolerant and kind   b) fair   c) intolerant   d) Spanish
11) What's the name of the Hindu lord who rebelled against Aurangzeb?
12) Write a paragraph to explain what the East India Company was.
13) When did Europeans start going to West Africa?
14) Write 3 sentences to explain how you think the growth of plantations in the West Indies and America affected the slave trade.
15) Explain why more than 11 million people died whilst being transported across the Atlantic to become slaves.
16) What was "The Underground Railroad"?
17) When was the Emancipation Proclamation, and what did it declare?
18) What is the 13th Amendment of the American Constitution?
19) What was the Ku Klux Klan?
20) Use three sentences to explain what segregation was, and how it affected people's everyday lives.
21) When was the Civil Rights Bill passed in America?
22) What is "propaganda"?
23) Name three ways the Jews were persecuted by the German Government after Hitler came to power.
24) Use three sentences to describe what you think the ghetto in Warsaw might have been like.
25) Write a paragraph to explain what happened to Anne Frank's family from July 1942 onwards.
26) What is "genocide"?
27) How many people were killed by the Nazis' "Final Solution"?
28) Who was put on trial at the Nuremburg Trials after WW2?
29) Write 3 sentences to say how technology changed warfare between WW1 and the end of WW2.
30) Why have civilians become more involved in wars?
31) How many people were killed by the two bombs dropped on Japan at the end of WW2?
32) Explain what the following terms mean:   a) Iron Curtain   b) the Cold War
33) What did Copernicus and Galileo both work out?
34) What was Charles Darwin most famous for writing about?
35) Say who the following people were and what their achievements were:   a) Louis Pasteur   b) Edward Jenner
36) What is the "Welfare State"?
37) When was the NHS introduced?

# Index

# Index